Curried Favors

FAMILY RECIPES FROM SOUTH INDIA

Curried Favors

FAMILY RECIPES FROM SOUTH INDIA

Maya Kaimal MacMillan

Food Photography by Brian Hagiwara
Location Photography by Zubin Shroff

ABBEVILLE PRESS PUBLISHERS
New York London Paris

For my father

FRONT COVER: Stir-Fried Shrimp with Green Beans Thoren. Photograph by Brian Hagiwara.
BACK COVER: *Clockwise from left:* Dried red chilies; ingredients for a South Indian curry; green beans and bananas; Cochin fish market. HALF-TITLE PAGE: *From left:* Ground red chili, turmeric, and coriander. FRONTISPIECE: Coconut palms near Alleppey, Kerala. Photographs by Zubin Shroff.

Studio food photography copyright © 1996 Brian Hagiwara
Location photography copyright © 1996 Zubin Shroff
Food styling by Anne Disrude
Prop styling by Betty Alfenito

EDITOR: Sarah Key
DESIGNER: Patricia Fabricant
TYPESETTER: Barbara Sturman
PRODUCTION EDITORS: Abigail Asher and Meredith Wolf
PRODUCTION MANAGER: Lou Bilka

First edition
10 9 8 7 6 5 4 3 2

Library of Congress Cataloging-in-Publication Data
MacMillan, Maya Kaimal.
    Curried favors : family recipes from South India / Maya Kaimal MacMillan.
        p. cm.
    Includes bibliographical references and index.
    ISBN 0-7892-0055-4
    1. Cookery, India—Southern style. 2. Cookery (Curry). I. Title.
TX724.5.I5M25 1996
641.5954′8—dc20   96-15281

ACKNOWLEDGMENTS

My deepest gratitude goes to my father, Chandran Kaimal, whose impeccable taste buds and pursuit of the reliable recipe made this book possible, and to my mother, Lorraine Kaimal, an excellent cook in her own right, who showed me that feeding others is as gratifying as eating well oneself. Thank you for everything.

I am indebted to my aunt, Kamala Nair, who took me into her kitchen and patiently explained so much. I'm also grateful to my grandmother, Ambuja Kaimal, whose legacy lives on in many of these recipes. And thanks to my cousins Padma, Mini, Ambika, and Sreelatha, who have inherited the skills of their mothers and kindly passed some of that knowledge on to me.

Many thanks to friends who have generously shared their culinary wisdom: Yoga Kalyanam, Mira Menon, Dev Raj Sikka, Indira Pradhan, Girija Ramanathan, Vanaja Parthasarathy, Latha Nair, Shashi Jones, Shashi Oonnithan, Saqlin, Prema Menon, Mrs. B. F. Varughese, and my aunt's skillful cook Pankajakshi Amma.

My heartfelt thanks go to those involved with the photography and design of this book: Zubin Shroff, Brian Hagiwara, Deborah Feingold, Anne Disrude, Betty Alfenito, and special thanks to my art director, Patricia Fabricant, for helping me fulfill a dream.

The guidance and encouragement provided by the following individuals is greatly appreciated: my editor Sarah Key, my agent Jane Dystel, Margo True, Scott Yardley, Susan Westmoreland, Susan Costello, Ellen Levine, and Florence Fabricant.

Finally, to my husband, James MacMillan, I am grateful beyond words. His affection, wisdom, and wonderful sense of humor are my sustenance.

Contents

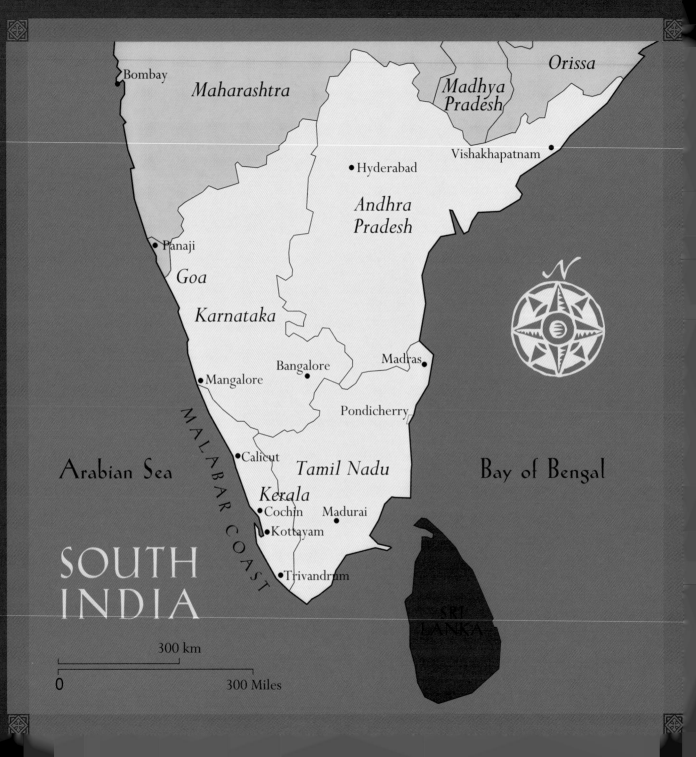

Bombay

Maharashtra

Orissa

*Madhya
Pradesh*

Vishakhapatnam

Hyderabad

*Andhra
Pradesh*

Panaji

Goa

Karnataka

Madras

Bangalore

Mangalore

Pondicherry

Arabian Sea

Calicut

Tamil Nadu

Bay of Bengal

Kerala

Cochin

Madurai

Kottayam

SOUTH
INDIA

Trivandrum

SRI
LANKA

300 km

0   300 Miles

Introduction

IF MY SOUTH INDIAN FATHER hadn't found himself in a Kansas wheat field thirty years ago, this book would never have been written. Because he was doing atmospheric research on the American prairie, miles from any restaurants, he tried his hand at cooking. Being a scientist gave my father an advantage in cooking—he liked to experiment, and he wrote everything down so he could duplicate his results. INSPIRED BY the flavors of his youth, he started with South Indian standards like *sambar,* a spicy lentil and vegetable stew; green bean *thoren* (green beans with coconut and mustard seeds); and *Mysore pak,* a shortbread-type sweet made with *ghee.* Dinners in my house would alternate between my American mother's forays into Julia Child and my father's latest experiments with Indian cooking. My sister and brother and I relished it all, and we were reminded of how good we had it when our school friends visited and, catching a whiff of lamb curry, asked if they could stay for dinner. JUST AS his trips to the Midwest tapered off, my father was approached by the owner of a cookware store in Boulder, Colorado, to see if he'd teach a course on Indian cooking. He taught the popular class for four years and continued refining more North and South Indian dishes all the while. As MY interest in cooking grew, I frequently found myself in the kitchen at his elbow— watching, learning, smelling, and tasting. While attending Pomona College in southern California, I formed a cultural club so I could make Indian food for my friends, and when I began working at a New York magazine I catered Indian dinners on deadline nights.

I was often struck by the disparity between the South Indian cooking I grew up with and the North Indian food served in restaurants. The more I cooked, the more I understood about different regional styles, and the more motivated I became to learn about South Indian food. Every few years our family would travel to Kerala, the state in South India where my father grew up. On these trips I would plant myself in my aunt's kitchen in her Kottayam home and take careful notes so I could try to reproduce those elusive flavors back in the U.S.

Kerala is an interesting and unique culinary pocket, its cuisine shaped by climate, geography, and religion. This tropical stretch of land extends along the Malabar Coast, where southwestern India meets the Arabian Sea. In the summer months the monsoon transforms it into a virtual rain forest. Coconut, fish, and shellfish are abundant there, and are combined in numerous curries including fish *molee* (fish with coconut milk and vinegar) and shrimp *thiyal* (shrimp in a toasted coconut sauce). Fragrant curry leaves (unrelated to curry powder) and mustard seeds,

Young girls along a canal in the Kerala backwaters

both of which grow in the region, distinctively season South Indian vegetable curries and *dhals* (split legumes). An extensive network of waterways outlines brilliant green rice paddies, rice being the staple starch in the diet.

In contrast, northern India, with its dry plains and cool temperatures, is ideal for growing wheat. The hard durum variety makes excellent *chappathi* (flat bread cooked on an iron skillet) and *puri* (deep-fried flat bread); consequently, breads make up the primary starch of that region. Milk products, including cream, *ghee* (clarified butter), and *paneer* (homemade cheese) all feature more prominently in the cooking of the north than that of the south.

While many of the same spices are used in both regions, they are manipulated differently in each. In the north they dry-roast whole spices before grinding them and adding them to their cooking; in the south they blend whole and powdered spices into a wet paste. To round out the flavor of a finished curry, North Indian cooks add a pinch of *garam masala*, a spice blend usually made with black pepper, cinnamon, cloves, and cardamom. In the south a curry is finished off with a seasoning of curry leaves, mustard seeds, and dried red pepper, sizzled together in coconut oil.

REGIONAL INFLUENCES

The southern tip of India was geographically isolated from the Mughal influence that took hold of the north in the Middle Ages. The Mughals were Central Asian invaders who filtered into India, establishing a dynastic rule that lasted from the sixteenth to the eighteenth century. They brought with them a taste for lamb, nuts, and dried fruits, and the forerunners of such contemporary North Indian staples as *tandoori* chicken and *pullao*. As Muslims, the Mughals avoided pork but ate other types of meat.

Prior to the arrival of the Mughals, Indian food attitudes in the north and the south were shaped by a Hindu belief that eating and spiritual advancement are part of the same cosmic cycle. Vegetarianism, and specifically avoiding beef, are aspects of this philosophy. The cow and bull have always had an auspicious place in the Hindu religion because of their close associations with the gods Krishna and Shiva, and an

Chinese fishing nets in Cochin harbor

important role in the economy as a source of milk and labor. And while Hindus would occasionally eat chicken, fish, goat, or lamb, Buddhists and Jains, on the other hand, followed a strict vegetarian lifestyle, which was relatively easy to do given India's natural abundance of vegetables, grains, and legumes.

Although the southern cuisine remained largely untouched by the Mughal influence, Kerala's wealth of black pepper, cinnamon, ginger, and turmeric turned the ports of Cochin and Calicut into magnets for the worldwide spice trade, bringing the region in contact with the Phoenicians, Romans, and Arabs throughout antiquity; Marco Polo in 1294; the Portuguese, including explorer Vasco da Gama, in 1498; and the Dutch and British beginning in the seventeenth century.

As each of these groups angled for a piece of the spice trade, they brought with them new foods that worked their way into the cuisine. Saffron, fennel, and fenugreek came originally from the Mediterranean, while New World tomatoes, potatoes, and cashews came to India by way of the Portuguese. The ingredient with the most dramatic impact on

Indian cooking was the chili pepper, first discovered by Columbus in the Caribbean, then brought to India by Portuguese traders. Until that point, Indian cooks relied on black pepper for pungency. Once the more complex-tasting chili arrived, it quickly replaced black pepper as the primary hot ingredient of the cuisine.

Since antiquity, the predominantly Hindu state of Kerala has been home to a thriving Christian population, some of whom St. Thomas the Apostle is believed to have converted in A.D. 52, some of whom arrived in the fourth century after fleeing persecution in Syria. This Syrian Christian community, which distinguishes itself by wearing only white, made a significant contribution to Kerala's cuisine, adding to the local fare meat dishes such as lamb stew and *piralen* (stir-fried meat marinated in vinegar and spices). The Christians eat all types of meat, including beef and pork. Today approximately 20 percent of Kerala's population is Christian, 60 percent is Hindu, and 20 percent is Muslim, and it is one of two states in India where slaughtering beef is legal (West Bengal is the other).

Among Kerala's Hindu population is a large

Indigenous to South India, black pepper growing on the vine

ancient subgroup called the Nayars (Nairs), to which my father belongs. Unlike the Namboodiris (Kerala's strictly vegetarian priest class), the Nayars eat chicken, fish, and lamb, although they never serve meat at wedding feasts. Certain dishes like *aviyal* (mixed vegetables cooked with coconut and tamarind) and *thoren* (shredded vegetables with grated coconut) are strongly associated with Nayar cooking.

The Muslim population in Kerala, called Moplas, descends from the Arab spice traders who frequented the Malabar Coast. The Muslims introduced elements of their own cooking to the south, with dishes like *biriyani,* an elaborate combination of rice and meat, and *kabab* (grilled marinated meat).

The cooking of Kerala has much in common with that of its neighboring South Indian states: Tamil Nadu, Karnataka, and Andhra Pradesh. Sharing similar climates, all four states incorporate coconut milk, tamarind, curry leaves, and mustard seeds into their dishes. The cooking in Tamil Nadu and Karnataka tends to be vegetarian, and *dosa* (fermented rice pancakes) and *sambar* are consumed in abundance. Andhra Pradesh's food is Muslim influenced, and renowned as the hottest food in India. Quintessential Kerala dishes, such as *appam* (rice and coconut pancakes), stew (coconut milk curries), and *kichadi* (chopped vegetables in a coconut and yogurt sauce), rely on the ever-present coconut. Nevertheless, few people know about the cuisine of these southern states because a majority of the Indian restaurants outside of India serve Mughal-style, North Indian food, since that is widely considered the most refined cooking in India.

If you *are* lucky enough to have a South Indian restaurant nearby, there's a good chance it's a vegetarian one. South Indian vegetarian restaurants have been successful in some urban areas, and it seems restaurant owners are reluctant to tamper with this formula. Furthermore, there is a perception among Indian restaurateurs that many of the common South Indian dishes like stews and *thorens* are rustic, homey foods that would not appeal to non-Indians. As a result, it is very difficult to find typical Kerala-style fish and meat curries outside of India. This book helps to fill that gap and at the same time provides some of the perennial North Indian favorites, like Rogan Josh (page 138), Spinach Paneer (page 81), and Eggplant Bhurta (page 96), that are enjoyed in North and South India alike. Taken together, these recipes give a sense of the wide array of flavors that make up Indian cuisine.

TIPS ON FINDING INGREDIENTS

A nice surprise is that most of the ingredients you'll need are sold in supermarkets. If not, they are available from local Indian, East Asian, or even Hispanic markets, or health food stores (see Notes on Ingredients, pages 17–24). For those not near international grocery stores, I've listed some mail-order sources in the back of this book (page 176).

You won't find references to commercial curry powder in any of these recipes. The terms "curry" and "curry powder" have become so generic that many people only have the vaguest sense of their meaning. "Curry powder" is not a single spice, and "curry" does not define a particular dish. A better definition of curry is a preparation of meat, fish, vegetables, eggs, or even fruit, cooked with a mixture of aromatic spices; it can be wet or dry, spicy or mild. Premixed, packaged "curry powder" doesn't allow for variety. If you want your dishes to be vibrant and distinctive tasting, blend your own spices for each recipe.

There are many possible origins for the word "curry": it could be from the Tamil (a South Indian language) word *kari,* meaning "sauce," or from *kari* leaves (or curry leaves, as I call them here) used in cooking in the south, or even from the wok-shaped vessel called a *kadhai*. These theories aside, we do know that the British took to using it in the eighteenth century as a general term for all the spicy Indian dishes they encountered, thus bringing it into common use.

If you keep some basic ingredients on hand—and you may already have them—it will take very little effort to use this book. You will need coriander, cumin, black pepper, red pepper (cayenne), turmeric, cinnamon, cloves, cardamom, mustard seeds (preferably brown), fennel seeds, and dried red chilies, all of which should be kept in airtight containers to preserve their flavors; anything more than two years old should be replaced. Some ingredients that may not be on your shelf are fresh green chilies, coconut milk, dried grated

"Seasoning" oil with mustard seeds, dried red peppers, and curry leaves

unsweetened coconut, curry leaves, and tamarind. Cooking with these ingredients will bring you much closer to replicating authentic flavors, so try to obtain them if possible. In some cases a substitution is suggested if the first choice is hard to find; in other cases exotic ingredients, like asafetida, are often listed as optional. In general, the more closely you follow the recipe, the more satisfying your results will be.

PREPARING AND SERVING INDIAN FOOD

The most efficient way to prepare an Indian meal is to have all the ingredients chopped and measured before beginning. This is useful because a common technique is to add various ingredients to a hot skillet in rapid succession. There will be a fair amount of chopping—everything is cut into bite-size pieces—so do that first. I recommend chopping generous batches of ginger and garlic and having them ready if you're making more than one recipe that needs them. It also helps to measure your ground spice mixtures into small bowls and have them ready to toss into the skillet.

A number of dishes require the use of green chilies. When handling chilies, be cautious. The oil in their seeds can cause a painful burning sensation, especially if it gets on your face or in your eyes. If you are extremely sensitive to chilies, you may wish to wear latex or rubber gloves. Always be sure to wash your hands thoroughly, and clean your knife and cutting surface when you're done.

One technique used throughout this book is "seasoning" oil with mustard seeds, curry leaves, and dried red peppers. This method is a standard part of

South Indian cooking—sometimes as the first step, sometimes as the last. In either case, it is advised that you have a lid over your skillet when heating the seeds, because as soon as they get very hot, they release their moisture and "pop." Allow the seeds to pop for about ten seconds (with the lid on) before proceeding to the next step in the recipe. This infuses the oil with a nutty flavor, which permeates the entire dish.

A few dishes call for only two or three spices, but generally curries need between five and ten aromatic ingredients to give them complexity. A spice blend in Indian cooking is referred to as a *masala,* which simply means a mixture of spices. Some recipes use dry *masalas*

A South Indian curry called kichadi *made with yogurt and topped with fresh curry leaves*

of ground spices, and some use wet *masalas* of ground spices worked into a paste with coconut, onion, and water. The consistency of the *masala* has no bearing on whether the final curry is wet or dry.

In the south, curries with plenty of sauce soak into mounds of rice or porous rice pancakes like *dosa* and are scooped up with the hand, while in the north drier curries picked up with small pieces of bread are favored. The Indian etiquette for eating with one's hand is to use the right hand only because the left hand is used for cleaning oneself, and therefore considered too impure to touch food. The right hand mixes rice, *dhal,* and curries together to form a moist ball and deftly pops it into the mouth or tears off a bit of bread and wraps it around a small amount of food.

Although eating with one's hand may seem unrefined to Westerners, there are strict rules governing it. When putting food in the mouth, for example, the hand should barely touch the mouth because contact with one's own saliva would "pollute" the rest of the food, and it is considered rude to lick the fingers while eating or to let pieces of rice drop from the hand. It's a simple art, mastered with a little practice.

Ideally, an Indian dinner should offer complementary flavors as well as contrasting colors and textures, consisting of at least three to four curries, salad, and rice. Based on that amount of food, I have provided each recipe with a suggested number of servings. If more than a few curries are prepared, each dish will stretch farther, and it follows that fewer dishes will not feed as many people.

The techniques involved in preparing Indian food are quite straightforward. After you've made a few dishes, it's easy to recognize the patterns in the seasoning and understand the principles behind the preparations. Omitting an ingredient is inadvisable the first time you try a recipe, and I especially caution you to adhere to the salt measurements. Salt makes it possible to taste the spices, and without it a curry will be utterly flat. In most recipes I have recommended tasting for salt before removing the curry from the heat. This step ensures that the saltiness is in balance with the hot (chilies and black pepper) and sour (lemon and tamarind) elements, a guideline taught to my father by his mother. According to my grandmother, if any one of these is in excess, the balance can be restored by slightly increasing the other two. The result will be a better balanced, albeit spicier, curry.

Coconut graters for sale; the serrated point is used to scrape the meat out of a coconut shell

Some recipes may seem to use a fair amount of oil. The quantity of oil in each recipe is based on the requisite amount needed for frying onions—about 2 tablespoons per cup (180g)—and for obtaining the proper flavor and consistency. Although the oil can be reduced with nonstick cookware, adhere to the recipes for the most authentic results.

A typical wet curry begins with frying onions over medium-high heat and stirring them frequently until the edges begin to caramelize and turn reddish brown. This can take up to twenty minutes. (Do not crowd too many onions in the pan because they will release so much water that the pan will never get hot enough to brown them. Fry in two batches if the pan is not very wide.) After the onions are browned, minced ginger and garlic are added and fried briefly, followed by the ground spices, the main ingredients, and the cooking liquid. The mixture is brought to a boil and then simmered for thirty to forty-five minutes. At the end of the cooking process the curry might be seasoned with *garam masala* or a combination of mustard seeds, curry leaves, and dried red peppers cooked in oil.

The recipes for dry curries begin with heating whole spices (mustard seeds or cumin seeds) in oil, adding the ground spices, the main ingredient, and a minimal amount of water—just enough to steam the meat or vegetable. Periodically a few drops of water are added so the curry won't dry out completely. Dry curries tend to cook faster than wet ones, especially *thorens,* which contain finely chopped or shredded vegetables.

Indian cooking is a family tradition; the same dish varies from region to region and home to home. These recipes come from my father, who acquired most of them from his family, and some from friends. After years of shaping, testing, and adapting these recipes with him, it is with pleasure that I pass this collection of Indian dishes along to you. So, when you're trying to curry favor with family and friends, begin with these uncomplicated recipes and unlock a new world of Indian flavors.

Equipment

You may already have all the cooking equipment needed to prepare an Indian meal. These are the items you will find yourself using frequently:

A set of sharp knives such as a 4-inch (10 cm) paring knife and two 6- to 9-inch (15 to 23 cm) utility knives

A wok with a lid for stir-frying dry curries and deep frying

One or two heavy-bottomed 4- to 6-quart (4 to 6 L) Dutch ovens or flameproof casseroles for wet curries—stainless steel, anodized aluminum, copper lined, or nonstick

Two 3-quart (3 L) saucepans with tight-fitting lids for rice and dhal—stainless steel, anodized aluminum, or copper lined

A heavy 10- to 12-inch (25 to 30 cm) nonstick frying pan with a lid, preferably with deep sides, for wet or dry curries

A food processor for grinding *masala* pastes, processing chutneys, and making dough

A mortar and pestle or coffee grinder dedicated to spices only

A complete set of measuring spoons and cups

A rolling pin for breads

A grater for preparing garlic, ginger, and onion to be used in marinades

Other useful items

A mini food processor for coarsely grinding whole spices and chopping garlic and ginger

A stainless-steel or aluminum *idli* stand, available at Indian grocery stores

Metal or wooden skewers for *kabab*

Cheesecloth (muslin) for making *paneer*

A small frying pan with a lid for seasoning oil with whole spices

An electric wok for controlled deep frying

A candy thermometer for deep frying and making sweets

Notes on Ingredients

Asafetida   This strong-smelling yellow powder has a name that means "fetid resin." It comes from the rhizomes, or underground stems, of several plants belonging to the parsley family. Asafetida is an important flavor component in *sambar* and *rasam,* and is also used to enhance rice dishes. Purchase it in powder form (sometimes under the name *hing*) in Indian and East Asian markets, in health food stores, and from mail order sources.

Atta Flour   For perfect *chappathi* and *puri,* nothing surpasses specially ground *atta* flour, also known as durum wheat flour. It is a low-gluten wheat that has been cultivated in India for thousands of years. If unavailable, substitute a mixture of two parts all-purpose flour and one part whole-wheat (wholemeal) flour. *Atta* is sold in Indian markets.

Bay Leaves   Dried bay leaves may be substituted for fragrant fresh curry leaves. A South Indian dish made with bay leaves instead of curry leaves won't taste as authentic, but will still taste good.

Black Pepper   Pepper vines are indigenous to the Malabar Coast of South India, and ground black pepper is made from dried unripened berries of these vines. Before chili peppers were brought to Asia from the New World in the sixteenth century, peppercorns provided the spicy element in Indian cooking. Pepper remains a key ingredient in the spice blends of most curries.

Black pepper

Clockwise from right: Grated coconut, ground red pepper, curry leaves, turmeric, coriander, and onions for a South Indian curry.

17

Cardamom This spice has often been called the "vanilla of India" because of its ubiquity in Indian desserts. Its fragrance also enhances meat and rice dishes. Cardamom pods form on the flower stalks of a plant related to ginger. The least processed form, the green seedpods, are preferred by most cooks. Bleached white pods and a ground form are also available. Both whole and ground cardamom are used in this book, and are available in supermarkets, Indian grocery stores, and health food stores.

Fresh green chilies

Cashew Nuts These sweet nuts were brought to India from Brazil by way of Portuguese traders. Today they are widely cultivated in India, frequently appearing in rice dishes and sweets. For cooking it's best to use broken raw cashews, available in health food stores and Indian grocery stores.

Chickpea Flour Also known as garbanzo flour or *besan*, this pale yellow flour is richer and more flavorful than wheat flour. It makes excellent batters for deep-fried snacks like *baji* and *pakora* and is also used to make the popular South Indian confection called *Mysore pak*. It is available in Indian grocery stores and health food stores.

Chilies, Fresh Chili peppers belong to the capsicum family and come in many shapes, sizes, and flavors. Fresh hot serrano chilies are the primary source of heat in curries, delivering a strong and resonant bite. Serranos are the width of a pencil and 3 to 4 inches (8 to 10 cm) long and come in shades of green and red. For Indian cooking look for green serranos, which are less ripe and therefore hotter than the red. If those are not available, look for tiny Thai chilies (also called bird's-eye chilies), which are thin, about an inch (2½ cm) long, and green or red in color, and substitute two Thai chilies for one serrano or one jalapeño. They are loaded with seeds and quite hot. If neither serrano nor Thai chilies are available, substitute plump, dark-green jalapeño peppers, which are about 2 inches (5 cm) long and milder. In the recipes in this book, chilies are either minced for a strong effect or split lengthwise for a gentler heat. If a somewhat mild curry is desired, remove the seeds before cooking; if a totally mild curry is desired, omit chilies entirely. Chilies are sold in many supermarkets; Indian, East Asian, and Hispanic grocery stores; and health food stores.

Cilantro or Fresh Coriander

The flavor of the leaves of the coriander plant (a member of the parsley family) is quite different from the flavor of the ground seeds. This fragrant, clean-smelling herb is used in a number of North Indian preparations. It should be added to a curry at the end of the cooking in order to retain its vibrancy. Cilantro can be purchased in supermarkets and in Indian, East Asian, and Hispanic markets.

Coconut

Cinnamon

Native to the hills of South India and Sri Lanka, cinnamon is the dried inner bark of a type of laurel tree. It is sold in supermarkets in rolled 2- to 3-inch (5 to 8 cm) sticks or as a powder. Both types are used in these recipes.

Cloves

A clove is the dried unopened flower bud of an evergreen tree native to Indonesia. In powder form it is used sparingly in meat curries, and as a whole spice it can add fragrance to rice dishes. Its sweet/hot taste has made it an ideal breath freshener since antiquity. This book calls for both the whole spice and the powder. It is available in supermarkets.

Coconut

In South India the abundant coconut palm has been called the "tree of life." The fruit, which constitutes a major part of the diet, yields a rich meat, milk, and oil. While freshly grated coconut meat is extremely flavorful, it requires a great deal of work to extract it from the shell. Alternatively, dried unsweetened grated coconut is available in health food stores or Indian and East Asian markets, and works very well. Be sure to look for finely grated coconut, not "powdered," which is too fine, or "shredded," which is too coarse. If all you can find is shredded coconut, process it finer in a food processor or blender. Store grated coconut in the freezer to prevent spoilage.

Coconut Milk

The creamy liquid extracted from grated coconut meat acts as a thickener in many South Indian gravies. It also adds an incomparable tropical flavor. Canned unsweetened coconut milk is an easily available substitute for fresh. Always stir the contents of the can thoroughly after opening because the oil collects at the top. Unused milk should be frozen. Canned coconut milk is sold in supermarkets and Indian, East Asian, and Hispanic markets. The regular type is preferable to the "light" variety, which makes curries very thin. If canned coconut milk is unavailable, use the recipe on page 171.

Coriander One of the most widely used seasonings in India, ground coriander seeds have a lemony aroma and act as a thickener in sauces. Only the ground form, not the seeds, is used in these recipes; it can be purchased in supermarkets, Indian markets, and health food stores.

Varieties of dhal *in Indian market*

Cumin Pale-green cumin seeds resemble caraway seeds and have a pleasant, unassertive flavor. North Indian cooks dry-roast whole seeds before grinding them, or use them whole to flavor cooking oil. In South Indian kitchens cumin is used in its unroasted ground form. It's useful to have both the seeds and the powder on hand. Cumin is available in supermarkets, Indian markets, and health food stores.

Curry Leaves No relation to curry powder, these highly aromatic, dark green leaves (also called *kari* leaves) grow on small trees native to South India. Sold in 8-inch (20 cm) sprigs with 10 to 20 leaves each, they give off a distinctly South Indian fragrance. In the South Indian kitchen, curry leaves are stripped off the stem, sizzled briefly in a bit of oil with brown mustard seeds and dried red chilies, and then stirred into a cooked dish. Alternately, the leaves can be added raw— along with some coconut oil (vegetable oil in this book)— at the end of cooking a curry. Curry leaves are sold at Indian and East Asian markets and are available from mail order sources.

Dhal The word refers to both the raw split legumes and the cooked dish. The smallish yellow *thoor* (or *thoovar*) *dhal* is the variety often used by Indian cooks. Similar to a lentil, it has an earthy flavor and cooks relatively quickly (30 minutes). Yellow or green split peas can be used instead, but take about 45 minutes to cook. Never add salt during the cooking process or the *dhal* will not soften completely. Split *urad dhal* (also called black gram) is called for in some recipes where it is browned in oil and added to rice or vegetable dishes to provide a bit of crunch. *Urad* and *thoor dhals* are sold in Indian markets and through mail order sources; yellow and green split peas are sold in supermarkets.

Farina

This ground-wheat product is featured in *rava dosa, rava idli, upuma,* and *sooji halva.* It is best known by its brand name Cream of Wheat and is available in supermarkets.

Fennel Seeds

These pale-green, ridged seeds look like fat cumin or caraway seeds. Their mild anise flavor makes them popular as a mouth freshener and digestive aid in India. Whole fennel seeds are crushed and added to meat, chicken, fish, and vegetable dishes, especially in the south. (Ground fennel is available but not used in any of the recipes in this book.) Fennel seeds can be found in supermarkets and Indian markets.

Fenugreek Seeds

Another essential ingredient in *sambar,* along with asafetida, is this strongly flavored seed. Sold whole in Indian markets and health food stores and through mail order sources, the seeds look like small amber-colored rectangles and are extremely hard. Either crushed or whole, the seeds are fried in oil before other ingredients are added to the pot.

Garam Masala

The Hindi term for this spice blend means "hot spices," and while the blend plays an essential part in North Indian cooking, it hardly appears at all in southern fare. Used sparingly, *garam masala* adds sparkle to meat and vegetable dishes after they have been cooked. In its most basic form it consists of black pepper for hotness and spices like cinnamon, cloves, and nutmeg for sweetness. Commercial varieties may also include roasted cumin and coriander. Making *garam masala* is quite simple, and a recipe is provided on page 171. Store-bought *garam masala* is less pungent, so use roughly twice as much.

Garlic, Fresh

Strict Hindu Brahmins consider garlic an aphrodisiac and therefore avoid it, but other Indians eat it in nearly every curry. Indeed, minced and fried with onion and ginger, garlic helps form the base of most wet curries. Grated garlic is used in meat marinades.

Ginger, Fresh

Considered the universal healer in *ayurveda,* or ancient Indian medicine, this rhizome, native to South India, is essential to most curries with garlic and onion. When used in marinades, it should be grated to eliminate the fibers. Fresh ginger is available in supermarkets, Indian and East Asian markets, and health food stores; when purchasing it, look for unwrinkled, supple-looking skin. Put the knobs in a jar and refrigerate, as they will dry out too much in the freezer. Ground dried ginger should not be substituted for fresh in these recipes.

Mace   The red-orange layer surrounding the nutmeg kernel is ground and sold as mace. In small amounts, with cinnamon and cloves, it imparts a rich aroma to meat dishes. Mace is sold in supermarkets, Indian and East Asian markets, and through mail order sources.

Fresh ginger

Mustard Seeds   Look for the small brown mustard seeds available at Indian grocery stores or through mail order. This variety has a nice aroma and a better taste than the yellow mustard seeds sold in supermarkets. In South India brown mustard seeds are sautéed briefly in oil with curry leaves and dried red peppers and then added to a curry to "finish" it, contributing a nutty flavor as well as a speckled appearance. When whole seeds are heated in oil, they pop as they release their moisture, making it important to use a lid for this process. When mustard seeds are crushed before being added to a curry, they provide a sour flavor.

Nutmeg   Nutmeg is the dried seed of an evergreen tree native to the Moluccas, or Spice Islands. It tastes similar to mace, the colorful coating around the nutmeg seed. It's easiest to purchase it ground at the supermarket; alternatively, buy whole seeds and use a nutmeg grater. In this book, tiny amounts are used with mace to flavor meat curries.

Oils   Coconut oil had always been the preferred all-purpose cooking oil in South India until concern about saturated fat led to a decrease in its consumption. Lighter vegetable oils like sunflower and corn oil are commonly used now. Actually, any mild-tasting oil is suitable for cooking South or North Indian food.

Onions   Indian onions resemble shallots, but I find shallots too much trouble to work with when large quantities are required. I use Spanish, or yellow, onions instead. Onions thicken Indian sauces without flavoring them with a strong onion taste. In most recipes they are sautéed until the edges turn reddish brown; never overcrowd the pan or they won't brown properly.

Poppy Seeds   Crushed poppy seeds are added to curries such as *rogan josh* to thicken the sauce. White poppy seeds are used in India, but the blue-gray European ones sold in supermarkets can also be used.

Red Pepper, or Cayenne This refers to the ground form of the dried ripe fruit of the capsicum family. Surprisingly, the ground red pepper used in India is milder than the kind sold in U.S. supermarkets. These recipes are calibrated to the hotter U.S. variety, so that ½ teaspoon is an ample amount for 8 people.

Whole dried red peppers

Red Peppers, Whole Dried To add extra piquancy to the seasoning of a dish, whole dried red peppers are tossed into hot oil with mustard seeds and curry leaves as a first step in cooking or to season a dish at the end. Breaking them in half will intensify this effect. They can be removed before serving since they are not eaten. Dried cayenne peppers, which are 1 to 2 inches (2½ to 5 cm) long, are sold in some supermarkets, and in Indian, East Asian, and Hispanic markets and through mail order. Other dried peppers of the same size may be substituted.

Rice Flour This finely ground, silky flour is excellent for making *appam* and *rava dosa*. It gives the pancakes their crisp texture. Rice flour is available in many supermarkets; Indian, East Asian, and Hispanic markets; and health food stores.

Rice, Long-Grain and Basmati Any regular long-grain white rice sold in supermarkets is suitable for eating with Indian food. Use this type for flavored rice dishes, except where noted. The aromatic basmati rice eaten in North India has a dry, light texture and nutty flavor. At Indian, East Asian, or health food stores (or mail order), look for the Dehra Dun type of basmati, which refers to a specific area in North India where the best crops are grown. Rice purchased from Indian or East Asian markets should be washed and picked over to remove particles before cooking. U.S.-grown varieties of basmati from Texas, called Texmati and Kasmati, are sold in supermarkets. Though pleasant in flavor, they are less aromatic than the Indian-grown type.

Saffron   Heralded for thousands of years for its color and fragrance, saffron comes from the dried stamens of crocus flowers and has always been the most expensive of all spices. Soak a tiny amount in hot milk for 15 minutes and add both infused milk and saffron to a meat curry, *pullao,* or dessert. Saffron is available in Indian, East Asian, or Hispanic markets and health food stores or through mail order.

Salt   Salt is an indispensable element in Indian cooking, and omitting it would seriously affect the balance of the seasonings. Always taste a dish for salt before serving. Oversalting can be counteracted with a few drops of lemon juice. The measurements in this cookbook are based on regular table salt, not coarse salt.

Tamarind   The juice of the tamarind pod is the sour element in many fish and vegetable curries in the south. Tamarind is sold as a soft block of pulp or as concentrate in a jar. The pulp requires boiling and draining; the concentrate is simply dissolved in hot water. Both forms are used in this book, because in those recipes where the taste of tamarind is foremost (Tamarind Chutney, Tamarind Fish), the pulp provides a nicer flavor. Tamarind is sold in Indian, East Asian, and Hispanic markets and health food stores or through mail order.

Thoor Dhal   *See* Dhal.

Turmeric   Its distinctive golden color has earned this rhizome a place in religious rituals and fabric dyeing as well as in cooking. It is the element that gives commercial curry powders their yellow cast. Turmeric can contribute nice color to a curry, but too much of it will cause a woody taste. Purchase ground turmeric in supermarkets.

Urad Dhal   *See* Dhal.

Yogurt   Made daily in Indian homes, fresh yogurt is served with a blanket of cream on top. It is used as a thickener for sauces and a base for *tandoori* marinade, and is a cooling element in salads. Every South Indian meal concludes with plain yogurt and rice to cleanse the palate. Plain low-fat (preferably) or nonfat yogurt may be used in these recipes.

Selling onions, potatoes, and garlic in Cochin

Light Meals and Savory Snacks

A TRADITIONAL SOUTH INDIAN BREAKFAST is a high-protein and high-carbohydrate affair, with split legumes and grains playing a major part. For those who choose to have "Western breakfast," there are meals of Indian-style eggs and toast. And no breakfast would be complete without strong Indian coffee. ◙ THE LIGHT FARE in this chapter includes not only breakfast specialties, but favorite snacks, and the wide range of legumes used in the snacks makes most of them high in protein as well. In India these savory refreshments would be enjoyed with afternoon tea, but feel free to serve them as hors d'oeuvres or first courses. ◙ IN THE SOUTH the quintessential breakfast food is *idli,* small, round steamed cakes of ground rice and *urad dhal* (small white split legumes), always served in pairs with coconut chutney and *sambar* (liquid lentil and vegetable curry). The batter for standard *idli* must be prepared the night before and fermented; however, the batter for Rava Idli (page 30), made with fried farina, is much simpler to prepare. Another widely enjoyed breakfast dish is Upuma (page 29), fluffy farina cooked with mustard seeds, cashew nuts, and onions. This spicy cereal tastes especially good with sliced bananas. ◙ TWO OTHER South Indian breakfast foods are *dosa* and *appam,* but when eaten with one or two curries these rice-based pancakes can also function as a lunch or light dinner. Traditional *dosa* are lacy crepes made from a thinner version of *idli* batter. Rava Dosa (page 32), on the other hand, are made with a

Front to back: Sambar, Rava Idli,
Coconut Chutney

27

combination of rice flour and farina, producing lovely light pancakes with the same faintly sour taste as regular dosa. The ever-popular masala dosa (dosa filled with potato curry) have become a favorite snack all over India, made with either plain *dosa, rava dosa,* or huge wafer-thin "paper" *dosa.* A version of this snack can be easily prepared with the Rava Dosa recipe (page 32) stuffed with Potatoes and Onions (page 86).

The most delicate South Indian pancake is the *appam,* also called a hopper, a delightfully sweet pancake of rice flour and coconut. Specially designed pans give *appam* thick centers and crisp golden edges. *Appam* are usually accompanied by curries made with coconut milk, like the lamb stew on page 129; the sweetness of the pancake complements the richness of the curry.

Eggs are enjoyed for a Western-style breakfast by nonvegetarians in North and South India alike. Usually served with coffee and slices of white toast, Spicy Scrambled Eggs (page 36) and Tomato and Onion Omelettes (page 37) are zesty starters.

Late afternoon is the time for socializing and snacking in most Indian homes. The daily ritual of afternoon tea with light fare was introduced to India by the British. Spicy snacks (pages 38–49) and sweetmeats (pages 157–69) evolved as India's answer to English sandwiches and tea cakes. In the coffee-rich southern states, teatime is often coffeetime, and well-known snacks called *vadas* and cool Coconut Chutney

(page 58) are served with it. Crunchy reddish-brown Split-Pea Vada (page 38) and batter-dipped Potato Vada (page 40) are delicious forms of this versatile favorite.

Some of the most popular savory tea snacks in India are deep-fried finger foods made with raw or cooked vegetables dipped in flavorful *besan* (chickpea flour) batters. In this category there are the crisp onion fritters known as Pakora (page 41), tempura-like batter-dipped vegetables called Baji (page 43), and South Indian spicy potato balls coated in batter called Bonda (page 42). Each fried snack should be paired with a chutney (pages 58–61) to round off its flavors. Perhaps India's best-known snack are the stuffed triangular pastries called samosas, and although sometimes filled with a ground meat mixture, the pea and potato version in this chapter (page 46) is more popular.

Since many of the following snacks require deep frying, here are a few guidelines for best results. Supply yourself with light vegetable oil, a wok, and a candy thermometer. The temperature for frying should be high enough (350° to 375°F; 180° to 190°C) to sear the surface instantly, ensuring that the food will not continue to absorb oil. Exceptions are Samosas and Split-Pea Vada, which require a longer cooking time at a lower temperature. Do not crowd the pan, or the temperature of the oil will drop too much and the food will not cook properly. Alternately, consider using an electric wok, which can maintain a steady temperature.

Upuma

Typically eaten for breakfast, upuma *(pronounced OOP-mah) is a little like couscous, with crunchy bits of fried cashew nut and* urad dhal *mixed in. First the* sooji *(farina or Cream of Wheat) is fried with seasonings until mostly cooked, then hot water is added, and the mixture is stirred briefly until it breaks into clumps. Serve with* ghee *and sliced bananas.*

¼ cup (30g) broken raw cashew nuts
1 tablespoon unsalted butter

2 tablespoons vegetable oil
1 tablespoon unsalted butter
½ teaspoon mustard seeds
1 tablespoon split urad dhal
1 dried red pepper, broken in half
10 curry leaves or 2 bay leaves
½ cup (85g) finely chopped onion
½ teaspoon minced ginger

1 cup (175g) farina (Cream of Wheat)
¾ teaspoon salt

1½ cups (355 ml) near-boiling water
1 teaspoon fresh lemon juice

2 bananas, thinly sliced
Ghee (page 172; optional)

In a wok over medium heat, fry cashews in 1 tablespoon butter until golden. Remove nuts from wok and set aside.

In the same wok wiped clean, heat oil, 1 tablespoon butter, mustard seeds, urad dhal, red pepper, and curry leaves or bay leaves, covered, over medium-high heat until mustard seeds begin to pop. Uncover, add onion and ginger, and stir until onion becomes soft but not browned.

Add farina and stir mixture over medium-high heat for 5 minutes until light golden brown. Stir in salt.

Slowly add near-boiling water and lemon juice and stir until farina has absorbed all the water. Turn heat down to medium and continue to stir for 30 seconds until mixture breaks apart into large lumps. Stir in reserved cashews. Remove from heat.

Serve with banana slices. A teaspoon of ghee with each serving will enhance the flavor.

PREPARATION TIME: 25 MINUTES   SERVES: 4

Rava Idli

 Steamed rice and lentil cakes called idli *(pronounced ID-lee), a popular breakfast food from South India, are high in protein and carbohydrates and have almost no fat. This version (pictured on page 26) with rava (farina or Cream of Wheat) has the same slightly sour flavor as traditional* idli *made from fermented rice and* urad dhal, *but is much easier and quicker to prepare. Steaming the* idli *requires an* idli *stand, or three-tiered aluminum steamer with depressions on each tier, or tray, to hold the batter; they are sold at Indian grocery stores. Serve hot with Coconut Chutney (page 58) and/or Sambar (page 68).*

½ teaspoon mustard seeds
1 teaspoon split urad dhal
1 tablespoon vegetable oil

10 curry leaves, coarsely chopped (optional)
1 teaspoon minced green chili (serrano,
　　Thai, or jalapeño)
1 cup (175g) farina (Cream of Wheat)
¾ teaspoon salt
¼ teaspoon baking soda (bicarbonate
　　of soda)

1⅓ cups (320 ml) plain low-fat yogurt
2 to 4 tablespoons water, as needed

Lightly oil depressions in idli trays.

In a covered wok or large frying pan, fry mustard seeds and urad dhal in oil over medium-high heat until mustard seeds begin to pop.

Add curry leaves and green chili and stir briefly. Add farina and fry, stirring constantly over medium-high heat for about 5 minutes, until farina turns golden. Add salt and soda and stir to combine thoroughly. Set aside to cool (see note).

Just prior to steaming, place farina mixture in bowl and stir in yogurt. Set aside for 2 minutes. If mixture is too thick to pour, add 2 to 4 tablespoons water. Spoon mixture into oiled depressions in idli trays. Batter should be thick but settle smoothly into place, almost filling each depression.

In a Dutch oven or flameproof casserole large enough to hold the stacked trays, bring an inch (2½ cm) of water to a boil. Place filled idli stand inside, cover, and steam for 10 to 12 minutes, or until cakes are cooked all the way through and no longer sticky inside. Remove from heat.

Antique bronze idli steamer

Using a pot holder, carefully remove idli stand from Dutch oven or casserole and set aside to cool for 2 minutes before removing cakes with a rubber spatula.

Note: The mixture can be prepared ahead of time up to this point and kept in the refrigerator for a week.

PREPARATION TIME: 40 MINUTES   SERVES: 4

YIELD: 12 CAKES

Rava Dosa

 Dosa *(pronounced DOE-sha) are South Indian crepes made from fermented lentil batter. The traditional method for making* dosa *requires soaking rice and* urad dhal, *grinding them into a batter, then fermenting the batter overnight at precisely the right temperature. Since it's tricky to get them right, I recommend this version made with wheat (rava) and rice flour, excellent* dosa *in their own right. The batter is a thin one that spreads easily. The final pancakes should have lots of small holes, giving them a lacy appearance. Cook* rava dosa *on a nonstick griddle or pan because they tend to stick to cast iron. In South India* dosa *are eaten with Sambar (page 68) and Coconut Chutney (page 58) as a snack. They could just as easily be served as a light lunch or dinner with Potato Stew (page 87) or Chicken Stew with Potatoes (page 117).*

1 cup (140g) rice flour
2 tablespoons all-purpose (plain) flour
½ cup (90g) farina (Cream of Wheat)
2 tablespoons minced onion
1 teaspoon minced ginger
1 teaspoon minced green chili (serrano,
   Thai, or jalapeño)
10 curry leaves, coarsely chopped (optional)
½ cup (120 ml) plain low-fat yogurt
1¼ teaspoons salt
2 to 2½ (480 to 600 ml) cups water

Vegetable oil for frying
Ghee (page 172)

In a medium bowl combine flours, farina, onion, ginger, green chili, curry leaves, yogurt, salt, and enough water to make a very thin batter. Cover and set aside for 1 hour at room temperature to rest.

In an 8- to 10-inch (20 to 25 cm) nonstick griddle or frying pan heat small amount of oil over medium heat until a light sprinkling of water sputters and crackles on surface of pan.

Before frying each dosa, stir batter well. It should be thinner than crepe batter, so it will spread easily on the griddle—add more water if necessary (see note). Ladle about ⅓ cup (80 ml) batter onto the hot griddle in a circular motion, starting from the outside and moving in, to make a thin pancake.

The pancake will be very thin, and as it cooks small holes will appear throughout. Sprinkle ghee generously on top. When bottom turns golden brown, turn pancake over and fry other side for 30 seconds.

Opposite: Rava Dosa

Serve folded in half, golden side out.

Note: Consistency of batter is critical to the success of dosa, so experiment with varying the amounts of water if necessary; if dosas come out thick and gummy, batter needs to be thinned.

PREPARATION TIME: 30 MINUTES,
PLUS 1 HOUR RESTING TIME   SERVES: 4 TO 6
YIELD: 12 PANCAKES

Rava Masala Dosa

 Masala dosa, *or rice and lentil crepes stuffed with potato curry, is one of the most popular snacks in India. Rava masala dosa (pictured on page 39) is simply the wheat-based version of the pancake. Here we make it by combining two easy recipes: Rava Dosa and Potatoes and Onions. Always serve it with Coconut Chutney (page 58) and Sambar (page 68).*

Rava Dosa (page 32)
Potatoes and Onions (page 86)

Prepare dosa batter an hour ahead of frying time. While batter is resting, prepare potatoes and onions as directed but break up potato pieces to make sure curry is thick.

Begin frying pancakes. Before removing each from pan (with golden side down), place about 3 tablespoons of potato mixture on one half, fold over like an omelette, and slide onto a warm platter. Keep in a warm oven while frying remaining pancakes. Do not stack or cover with a lid, or they will become soggy.

PREPARATION TIME: 1 HOUR 30 MINUTES,   SERVES: 4 TO 6
INCLUDING RESTING TIME FOR BATTER

YIELD: 12 FILLED PANCAKES

Light Meals and Savory Snacks ▨ 33

Appam

One of my favorite Kerala specialties, these delightfully sweet rice-flour pancakes (pictured on page 89) have a thick center and a crisp golden brown edge. In India there is a special pan designed for cooking appam *that looks like a small wok with a deeper, more pointed center. The shape of the pan gives the pancake a distinctly thick middle. Use an 8-inch (20 cm) nonstick frying pan and tilt it so the edge of the pancake is thin and the center remains relatively thick. While the shape may not be perfectly authentic, the flavor is.* Appam *are best served with Potatoes and Onions with Tomato (page 88) and any of the stews, as the flavor of their coconut milk gravies complements the pancakes' sweetness. To speed up the process, have two pans going at the same time.*

1½ teaspoons active dry yeast
1 tablespoon sugar
⅓ cup (80 ml) lukewarm water
¾ cup (85g) grated unsweetened coconut

¼ cup (35g) cream of rice cereal
2¼ cups (530 ml) water
1¾ cups (240g) rice flour
¼ teaspoon salt
2 tablespoons sugar
1 cup (240 ml) canned unsweetened
　coconut milk
Water, as needed

Prepare batter the night before you plan to serve appam. Dissolve yeast and 1 tablespoon sugar in lukewarm water. Set aside for 5 minutes or until foamy. In a blender or mini food processor grind coconut to a fine powder; set aside. (Texture will not be fine enough in a regular food processor.)

Cook cream of rice with ¾ cup (180 ml) water in a small saucepan over medium heat until a thick porridge forms. In a large bowl combine cooked cream of rice, ground coconut, and rice flour with remaining 1½ cups (360 ml) water. Whisk together to form a thick batter. Add dissolved yeast mixture, salt, and 2 tablespoons sugar and blend thoroughly. Keep in a warm place overnight, such as a pilot-lit oven with a large bowl of very hot water.

The next day batter will have risen or appear bubbly from fermentation. When you are ready to begin frying, stir in coconut milk and a few tablespoons of water, as needed, to form a thin batter the texture of heavy cream. The batter may thicken over time, in which case a tablespoon or two

Carved door of an old Kerala home

of water should be added to maintain a thin consistency. Sprinkle a few drops of vegetable oil in an 8- to 10-inch (20 to 25 cm) nonstick frying pan over medium heat. When pan is hot, stir batter well and pour in a scant ⅓ cup (80 ml) of batter. After a moment, lift pan and tilt in a circular motion to spread batter to a 7-inch (18 cm) diameter. Pancake should be thin and "lacy" around edges and thicker and opaque white in the center. Cover and cook for 3 to 5 minutes. Do not flip over! Appam is done when lightly browned around edges and center is dull looking and dry to the touch (see note). Remove pancake by running spatula around edges and sliding onto a platter. Keep platter in a warm oven while preparing remaining pancakes, placing pancakes on platter in oven as they are cooked.

Serve immediately.

Note: Test to see if appam is cooked through; if browned but sticky in the center, batter is too thick.

PREPARATION TIME: 20 MINUTES TO PREPARE BATTER;
12 HOURS MINIMUM TO FERMENT;
50 MINUTES FOR FRYING   SERVES: 6 TO 8
YIELD: 20 PANCAKES

Spicy Scrambled Eggs

 This is a refreshing change from regular scrambled eggs. Control the hotness by adjusting the amount of green chili.

10 extra-large eggs
¼ to ½ teaspoon salt
¼ teaspoon ground black pepper

½ teaspoon cumin seeds
2 tablespoons vegetable oil
1 cup (180g) finely chopped onion
1 to 1½ teaspoons minced green chili
   (serrano, Thai, or jalapeño)
2 tablespoons unsalted butter

In a large bowl whisk together eggs, salt, and pepper; set aside.

In a large nonstick frying pan over medium heat, fry cumin seeds in oil. When seeds begin to brown and give off their aroma, add onion and green chili and sauté until onion softens.

Pour contents of skillet into egg mixture and stir to combine.

In the same skillet melt butter over medium to medium-low heat. Add eggs and cook, stirring constantly and gently, until eggs are cooked but still moist.

PREPARATION TIME: 30 MINUTES   SERVES: 6

View of a canal in Kerala

Tomato and Onion Omelettes

 These omelettes have onion and green chili mixed into the eggs, and are then stuffed with tomato and cilantro. You could also fill them with a little leftover vegetable or meat curry.

10 extra-large eggs
½ teaspoon salt
⅛ teaspoon ground black pepper

1 cup (180g) finely chopped onion
1½ teaspoons minced green chili (serrano, Thai, or jalapeño)
2 tablespoons vegetable oil

1 cup (225g) finely chopped, seeded tomato
¼ cup (15g) chopped cilantro (fresh coriander)

In a bowl combine eggs, salt, and pepper; set aside.

In a small nonstick frying pan over medium-high heat, sauté onion and chili in oil until soft. Add onion to eggs; stir to combine.

Set same skillet (or an omelette pan) over medium heat, using any oil remaining in the pan, or adding ½ teaspoon of oil to the omelette pan. When hot, add ½ cup (120 ml) of egg mixture. Cook until surface doesn't jiggle when shaken but still appears shiny. Sprinkle some tomato and cilantro on one half, then flip plain side of omelette over filling. Underside should be slightly brown. Slide omelette onto a platter and place in warm oven. Add ½ teaspoon oil to pan and repeat until egg mixture and filling are used up.

PREPARATION TIME: 30 MINUTES   SERVES: 6 TO 8
YIELD: EIGHT 6-INCH (15 CM) OMELETTES

Split-Pea Vada

Vada are South Indian fried snacks often made from dhal-*based batters. The granular batter produces crisp, reddish-brown patties with a rough surface. Serve with Coconut Chutney (page 58) as an appetizer or afternoon snack. A food processor works better than a blender as it requires less water for grinding* dhal.

1 cup (180g) thoor dhal or yellow split peas

⅓ cup (80 ml) water

¾ cup (130g) finely chopped onion
½ teaspoon minced garlic
½ teaspoon minced green chili (serrano, Thai, or jalapeño)
⅛ teaspoon fennel seeds, coarsely ground with a mortar and pestle
⅛ teaspoon ground cumin
⅛ teaspoon ground red pepper (cayenne)
⅛ teaspoon asafetida (optional)
¾ teaspoon salt

Vegetable oil for deep frying

Rinse thoor dhal or yellow split peas and soak in 1 quart (950 ml) water for at least 4 hours.

Drain dhal thoroughly. In a food processor or blender combine with ⅓ cup (80 ml) water and process to form a coarse mixture but not a paste. A small clump should be easily pressed into a ball without falling apart.

Transfer ground dhal to a medium bowl. Add onion, garlic, chili, spices, and salt and mix well. Form into patties 1½ inches (4 cm) in diameter and ⅜ inch (1 cm) thick by pressing into palm of one hand. Make patties promptly, or liquid will separate out. Set aside.

In a wok or deep saucepan heat oil to 325° to 350°F (165° to 180°C). Cooking 5 or 6 at a time, deep-fry patties until they turn a dark reddish color (about 5 minutes; see note). Remove with slotted spoon to paper-towel-lined platter to drain. Keep in a warm oven while frying remaining patties.

Note: Patties are thick in the center; break apart one from first batch to be sure they are cooking all the way through.

PREPARATION TIME: 45 MINUTES, PLUS 4 HOURS SOAKING TIME
SERVES: 4 TO 8
YIELD: 20 PATTIES

Opposite (clockwise from top): Coconut Chutney, Split Pea Vada, Rava Masala Dosa, Spiced Tea

Potato Vada

The vada in this recipe, from my grandmother, consist of flat potato cakes dipped in an egg batter and briefly deep fried. Eat them promptly or they will become soggy. Serve with Coconut Chutney (page 58).

4 medium boiling potatoes, peeled and
    quartered
Salt

1½ cups (250g) finely chopped onion
3 tablespoons vegetable oil

1 teaspoon minced ginger
1 teaspoon minced green chili (serrano,
    Thai, or jalapeño)
½ teaspoon salt

1 cup (240 ml) water
1 large egg, lightly beaten
½ teaspoon salt
1 cup (140g) all-purpose (plain) flour

Vegetable oil for deep frying

In a saucepan of salted water boil quartered potatoes for 12 to 15 minutes until just tender. Drain and mash thoroughly.

In a medium frying pan over medium heat, fry onion in oil until soft.

In a large bowl combine mashed potatoes, sautéed onion, ginger, green chili, and ½ teaspoon salt and mix thoroughly. Using your hands, press mixture into flat cakes 2 inches (5 cm) in diameter and ½ inch (1½ cm) thick. Set aside.

In a small bowl beat water, egg, and salt to blend. Stir into flour in a separate bowl to prepare medium-thin batter.

In a wok or deep saucepan, heat oil to 350° to 375°F (180° to 190°C). Dip cakes into batter and deep-fry, about 5 at a time, until golden. Remove with slotted spoon to paper-towel-lined platter to drain. Keep in warm oven while frying remaining cakes.

PREPARATION TIME: 50 MINUTES   SERVES: 4 TO 8
YIELD: 26 TO 30 CAKES

Pakora

These spicy fritters are made of chopped onion, ginger, and spices mixed into a thick chickpea-flour (besan) batter. They are different from the baji of the following recipe in that the onion is finely chopped and mixed into the batter, and the fritters come out in irregular shapes. Serve with Coconut Chutney (page 58) or Cilantro and Mint Chutney (page 60).

2 cups (280g) chickpea flour, sifted

2 cups (360g) finely chopped onion

2 teaspoons minced ginger

2 teaspoons minced green chili (serrano,
    Thai, or jalapeño)

½ teaspoon ground red pepper (cayenne)

¼ teaspoon ground turmeric

¼ teaspoon asafetida (optional)

½ teaspoon baking powder

1½ teaspoons salt

½ to 1 cup (120 to 240 ml) water, as needed

Vegetable oil for deep frying

In a medium bowl mix flour, onion, ginger, chili, spices, baking powder, salt, and water to make a thick batter that drops off your fingers in clumps.

Heat oil to 350°F (180°C). Using your hand or a spoon, scoop up a small amount of batter (about a tablespoon) and drop it into hot oil so it forms a 1 to 1½-inch (2½ to 4 cm) clump. Fry 5 or 6 at a time until golden brown, then remove with slotted spoon to paper-towel-lined platter to drain. Keep in warm oven while frying remaining fritters.

PREPARATION TIME: 30 MINUTES   SERVES: 6 TO 8

Bonda

A popular South Indian snack, these zesty potato balls are dipped in a well-spiced chickpea (besan) *and rice-flour batter and fried.* Urad dhal *in the filling gives them some crunch inside. As with all batter-fried snacks, eat them promptly. Serve warm, with Coconut Chutney (page 58).*

Salt

3 medium boiling potatoes, peeled and
  cut into 1-inch (2½ cm) cubes

1 teaspoon mustard seeds
2 tablespoons split urad dhal
3 tablespoons vegetable oil

1 cup (180g) finely chopped onion
2 teaspoons minced ginger
1 teaspoon minced green chili (serrano,
  Thai, or jalapeño)
¼ to ½ teaspoon salt

⅔ cup (100g) chickpea flour, sifted
⅓ cup (50g) rice flour
¼ teaspoon ground red pepper (cayenne)
⅛ teaspoon ground turmeric
⅛ teaspoon asafetida (optional)
¾ teaspoon salt
¾ cup (180 ml) water, as needed

Vegetable oil for deep frying

In a medium saucepan of salted water, boil cubed potatoes until tender. Drain; return to saucepan and break up with potato masher to coarse, slightly chunky texture.

In a covered wok or large frying pan heat mustard seeds and urad dhal in oil over medium-high heat, until mustard seeds begin to pop and urad dhal turns light brown.

Uncover and stir in onion, ginger, green chili, and ¼ to ½ teaspoon salt. Sauté for 1 minute. Add potato and stir for 2 minutes. Mixture should be partially mashed and moist enough to form balls. Remove from heat.

When cool, carefully press potato mixture into firm 1-inch (2½ cm) balls, using the palm of one hand. Balls should be compact and smooth. Set aside.

In a bowl combine flours, red pepper, turmeric, asafetida, salt, and water as needed to make a moderately thick batter, like pancake batter.

In a wok or deep saucepan, heat oil to 365° to 375°F (185° to 190°C). Dip potato balls in batter and fry, 5 or 6 at a time, until golden brown. Remove with a slotted spoon to paper-towel-lined platter to drain. Keep in warm oven while frying remaining balls.

PREPARATION TIME: 45 MINUTES   SERVES: 6 TO 8
YIELD: ABOUT 30 BALLS

Baji

 These batter-dipped fried vegetables are enjoyed all over India. The batter, like that of pakora, *is made of chickpea flour* (besan), *but it is thinner. Onion and eggplant (aubergine) are our favorite for making this snack, but you can also use potato or zucchini (courgette). Slice very thin for best results. Serve hot, with Coconut Chutney (page 58) and Cilantro and Mint Chutney (page 60).*

1 cup (140g) chickpea flour, sifted
¼ teaspoon ground red pepper (cayenne)
⅛ teaspoon ground turmeric
⅛ teaspoon asafetida (optional)
¾ teaspoon salt
¾ cup (180 ml) water, as needed

Vegetable oil for deep frying
1 of each: onion, small Italian eggplant
(aubergine), potato, and small zucchini
(courgette) cut into ⅛-inch (½ cm)
cross-sections

In a small bowl mix flour, spices, salt, and water to medium-thin batter.

In a wok or deep saucepan heat oil to 350°F (180°C). Dip vegetable slices in batter and deep-fry, in batches, at 350°F (180°C) to a golden brown. Remove with slotted spoon to paper-towel-lined platter to drain. Keep in warm oven while you fry remaining vegetables.

PREPARATION TIME: 30 MINUTES   SERVES: 6

Meat Cutlets

 Cutlets, or meat and vegetable patties dipped in bread crumbs and fried, are a British-Indian specialty probably derived from croquettes. Try serving them as a first course with Spicy Tomato Chutney (page 61) or Tomato and Onion Salad (page 56).

Salt

2 medium boiling potatoes, peeled and cut into 1-inch (2½ cm) cubes (about 2 cups; 340g)

1 cup (180g) finely chopped onion
1 tablespoon vegetable oil
3 teaspoons minced ginger
2 teaspoons minced green chili (serrano, Thai, or jalapeño)

1 pound (450g) very lean ground beef (or lamb)
1¼ teaspoons salt

1 large egg white
1 teaspoon water
⅔ cup (70g) plain dry bread crumbs

⅔ cup (160 ml) vegetable oil, as needed

In a small saucepan of salted water, boil cubed potato until potatoes are very tender (8 to 10 minutes). Drain; return to saucepan and break up with a potato masher to a coarse, slightly chunky texture.

In a large frying pan over medium heat, fry onion in oil until it softens and begins to turn translucent. Add ginger and green chili and stir for 1 minute.

Raise heat to medium-high, add ground meat and salt, and stir until the meat's pink color disappears but before meat begins to release its liquid. Remove from heat and drain off any juices.

Add mashed potatoes to meat and combine thoroughly. When mixture is cool enough to handle, form into 2-inch (5 cm) balls. Press each ball into a flat oval cake about 2 inches (5 cm) in diameter and ¾ inch (2 cm) thick. Edges should be smooth and firm with no cracks, to prevent crumbling when frying.

In a shallow bowl whisk egg white and water together. Spread bread crumbs in second shallow bowl. Dip each cake in egg white, then roll in bread crumbs to coat.

When all cakes are ready, heat oil in a large frying pan over medium heat. When oil is hot, fry 6 at a time until well browned on both sides. The cakes should be covered with a crisp brown crust. Remove with slotted spoon to paper-towel-lined platter to drain. Keep in warm oven while frying remaining cakes.

PREPARATION TIME: 45 MINUTES   SERVES: 6 TO 8
YIELD: 12 CAKES

Shami Kabab

 These spiced meat patties are a favorite North Indian snack from Punjab. Serve with Chutney for Kabab (page 61) and lime wedges.

1 pound (450g) very lean ground beef
   (or lamb)
2 teaspoons all-purpose (plain) flour
2 tablespoons finely grated onion
2 teaspoons finely grated ginger
1 teaspoon finely grated garlic
1 teaspoon minced green chili (serrano,
   Thai, or jalapeño)
2 tablespoons finely chopped cilantro (fresh
   coriander)
1 teaspoon salt
Spice mixture
   ¼ teaspoon ground red pepper (cayenne)
   ¼ teaspoon ground black pepper
   ⅛ teaspoon ground cloves
   ⅛ teaspoon ground cinnamon
1 teaspoon fresh lime juice

Vegetable oil for frying

In a medium bowl combine ground meat, flour, onion, ginger, garlic, chili, cilantro, salt, ground spice mixture, and lime juice. Mix thoroughly and knead in the bowl for a minute or two. Form into 1½-inch (4 cm) balls, then flatten into patties ½-inch (1½ cm) thick.

In a lightly oiled nonstick frying pan over medium heat, fry patties until browned on both sides and no longer pink in center. Serve hot.

PREPARATION TIME: 40 MINUTES   SERVES: 6
YIELD: 12 PATTIES

Samosas

 This vegetable version of the well-known North Indian savory snack (pictured on page 50) contains potatoes and peas wrapped in a pastry and deep-fried. Tasty hors d'oeuvres for parties, they can be prepared ahead of time except for frying. Keep stuffed samosas covered and begin frying them 30 minutes before serving. Serve with Cilantro and Mint Chutney (page 60) or Tamarind Chutney (page 59).

2 cups (280g) all-purpose (plain) flour
½ teaspoon salt
⅓ cup (80 ml) vegetable oil
½ cup (120 ml) water, as needed

2 medium boiling potatoes, peeled and cut
   into ¼-inch (¾ cm) dice (about 2 cups;
   340g)
Salt

1 teaspoon cumin seeds
¼ cup (60 ml) vegetable oil
1 cup (180g) finely chopped onion
2 teaspoons finely minced ginger
½ teaspoon minced green chili (serrano,
   Thai, or jalapeño; optional)
1 teaspoon ground coriander
½ teaspoon Garam Masala (page 171)
⅛ teaspoon ground red pepper (cayenne)
1 teaspoon salt

1 cup (135g) frozen peas
Water, as necessary
2 tablespoons finely chopped cilantro
   (fresh coriander)
1 tablespoon fresh lemon juice

Vegetable oil for deep frying

Prepare pastry for samosas by combining the flour, salt, and oil thoroughly, or by rubbing with fingers in a large bowl. Gradually add water, a little at a time, until mixture forms into a ball. Knead briefly to form a smooth, slightly elastic dough. Place in a bowl, cover, and let stand for 30 minutes.

While dough is resting, prepare filling. In a medium saucepan of well-salted water, boil potatoes until tender. Drain and set aside.

In a large, deep pan over medium-high heat, heat cumin seeds in oil until seeds begin to turn a light brown. Uncover, add onion and ginger, and fry until onion turns light brown. Add the green chili, coriander, garam masala, red pepper, and 1 teaspoon salt, and stir for another minute.

Stir in peas and fry until the peas are cooked but still bright green. Add a small amount of water, if necessary, to prevent spices from sticking. Stir in reserved potatoes and cook for 2 minutes, stirring frequently. Add cilantro and lemon juice and remove from heat. Let mixture cool before proceeding.

*Street vendor selling fried bananas (foreground)
and samosas (left)*

Knead dough a few times, then divide into 12 balls. Roll
each ball out to a very thin, 6-inch (15 cm) circle. Cut one
circle in half and form a cone by folding the cut side in half,
overlapping it ¼ inch (¾ cm) and sealing the overlap with
a little water. Place about a tablespoon of potato filling in
bottom of cone; do not overfill or pastry will burst. Close
top of cone with at least a ¼-inch (¾ cm) overlap, using
water to seal edges. You can decoratively pinch top closed
(like an empanada) or press with tongs of a fork to strengthen
the seal. Completely seal dough, or it will leak when fried.

In a wok or deep saucepan, heat oil to 350°F (180°C) and
fry samosas, 6 at a time, maintaining heat around 325°F
(165°C), about 5 minutes, or until pastry turns golden
brown (long frying time gives pastry a tender texture).

Remove with a slotted spoon to paper-towel-lined platter to
drain. Keep in warm oven while frying remaining samosas.

PREPARATION TIME: 1 HOUR 15 MINUTES   SERVES: 8 TO 12
YIELD: 24 SAMOSAS

Nimki

These tasty strips are perfect to nibble on with drinks before dinner. Nimki *can be prepared in very little time, especially if oil for deep frying is already heated for* pappadam *or* puri. *Be sure to roll the dough out very thin or the* nimki *will be doughy instead of crisp. Serve plain or with Tamarind Chutney (page 59).*

1 cup (140g) all-purpose (plain) flour
1 tablespoon vegetable oil
½ teaspoon salt
¼ teaspoon baking powder
1 teaspoon cumin seeds
1 teaspoon sesame seeds
¼ to ⅓ cup (60 to 80 ml) water, as needed

Vegetable oil for deep frying

In a medium bowl mix flour, oil, salt, baking powder, cumin seeds, sesame seeds, and water, starting with ¼ cup (60 ml), to make a stiff dough. Add more water sparingly if too dry.

Knead dough a few times and divide into 2-inch (5 cm) balls. Roll balls into circles 1/16 inch (¼ cm) thick, then cut circles into strips 2 to 3 inches (5 to 7½ cm) long and ⅜-inch (1 cm) wide. Deep-fry strips, in two or three batches, in 350°F (180°C) oil until golden brown.

PREPARATION TIME: 30 MINUTES   SERVES: 8 TO 12

Pappadam

Also called papad, *these crispy wafers made from* urad dhal *are purchased raw and then cooked at home. In the north they are roasted, but in the south they are deep-fried.* Pappadam *(pictured on page 126) can be served as a snack dipped in chutney. In my aunt's home we crumble them up and mix them with our rice and curries to add a crunchy texture and earthy flavor.*

12 pappadam, broken into half circles if over 6 inches (15 cm) in diameter (available at Indian grocery stores)
Vegetable oil for deep frying

In a large wok heat oil to 350°F (180°C), hot enough for a small piece of pappadam dropped in to expand quickly and rise to the top.

Fry pappadam, one at a time, in hot oil. They will expand immediately and should cook to a golden color in about 3 to 5 seconds (see note). Remove from oil with tongs and drain on paper towels.

Note: If pappadam turn reddish brown, temperature is too high or they have been cooked too long. If they look oily even after draining and take longer to cook, temperature is too low.

PREPARATION TIME: 15 MINUTES
SERVES: 8 TO 12, DEPENDING ON SIZE OF PAPPADAM

Pappadam

Soups, Salads, and Chutneys

THIS CHAPTER OFFERS simple side dishes to enhance any meal. Soups and salads were Western imports, but once they hit the subcontinent they acquired a distinctively Indian twist. Simple and versatile, these dishes can also add sparkle to non-Indian menus. Chutneys are zesty Indian relishes that come in various forms. The chutneys here are best eaten with the savory snacks on pages 27–49. ▨ Soups are not traditionally Indian. Mulligatawny Soup (page 55) was originally created for the British in India who felt the need for a soup course. Based on *rasam,* a spicy lentil broth with onions and tomatoes, it has appeared in various forms over the last two hundred years, including the version here with coconut milk. Rasam Soup (page 53) and Pulisheri Soup (page 54), made of buttermilk with cucumber and curry leaves, are actually South Indian curries that are usually eaten spooned over a pile of rice. Their liquid consistency makes them ideal soups. ▨ Salads can be either cool foils to a spicy meal or side dishes spiced with fresh green chili. Lightly cooked vegetable and yogurt dishes like *pachadi* and *kichadi* are sometimes considered "salads" in India, but this chapter includes only salads made from raw vegetables. Some raw salads consist of vegetables and seasonings folded into a creamy yogurt base, like cucumber Raita (page 57) and Ginger Yogurt (page 57). Others, like the Tomato and Onion and Tomato and Cucumber Salads (page 56) are vibrantly dressed with lemon juice or vinegar and green chili. Reducing or

Clockwise from top: Tomato and Onion Salad,
Samosas, Pulisheri Soup, Tamarind Chutney,
Cilantro and Mint Chutney

Tomato vendor

omitting the green chili will yield a mild salad. If a salad is prepared ahead of time, add the salt just before serving to prevent it from becoming watery.

Chutneys are uniquely Indian. These spicy, sweet, or sour relishes have been a feature of Indian cuisine for centuries, providing the full spectrum of tastes to an Indian meal. Among the many forms of chutneys are those made from fresh herbs (like Cilantro and Mint Chutney on page 60) or fruits or vegetables cooked with spices (like Tamarind Chutney and Spicy Tomato Chutney on pages 59 and 61). Coconut Chutney (page 58) is the most popular chutney in South India. Its creamy, spicy qualities make it perfect with snacks like *idli, dosa, pakora, vada,* and *bonda* (see the preceding chapter). Raw chutneys should be eaten the day they are made, but cooked ones will keep for about two weeks in the refrigerator.

The chutneys mentioned above are intended to be eaten with snacks, but in India the term *chutney* includes pickles made from green mango, lemon, and gooseberry, to name just a few. After being preserved for months in hot spices and vinegar, these mixtures yield very pungent relishes eaten in tiny quantities along with curries, rice, and yogurt. The British found that preserved chutneys traveled well, and not only did they perk up a long sea voyage, they also became quite popular in England.

Rasam Soup

 A zesty lentil broth from Tamil Nadu, rasam *gets its distinct flavor from fenugreek, asafetida, and curry leaves. It was the closest thing to soup that the British could find in India, and they used it to develop the more elaborate mulligatawny soup. I suggest serving this toned-down version of* rasam *as a spicy first course.*

¼ cup (45g) thoor dhal or yellow split peas
1 cup (240 ml) water
⅛ teaspoon ground turmeric

½ teaspoon mustard seeds
½ teaspoon cumin seeds
⅛ teaspoon fenugreek seeds
20 curry leaves or 4 bay leaves
2 tablespoons vegetable oil
¼ teaspoon asafetida
2 cups (450g) chopped tomatoes, fresh or
    canned, drained
1 green chili (serrano, Thai, or jalapeño),
    split lengthwise (optional)
¼ teaspoon Sambar Spice Blend (page 170)
2¼ teaspoons salt

4 cups (960 ml) water

5 sprigs cilantro (fresh coriander), leaves only
4 teaspoons fresh lemon juice

In a 2-quart (2 L) or larger saucepan, bring thoor dhal (or split peas), 1 cup (240 ml) water, and turmeric to boil. Turn down heat and simmer, partially covered, for about 30 minutes until dhal is very soft (about 45 minutes for split peas). Mash dhal thoroughly, in saucepan, with potato masher or back of a spoon. Set pan aside.

In a small covered frying pan heat mustard, cumin, and fenugreek seeds and curry leaves in oil over medium-high heat, until mustard seeds begin to pop. Uncover, add asafetida, and stir very briefly. Add tomatoes, green chili, spice blend, and salt and stir over medium-high heat for 1 minute.

Add tomato mixture to cooked dhal in saucepan. Add 4 cups (960 ml) water and bring to a boil. Turn down heat and simmer, partially covered, for 30 minutes until tomatoes completely break down and mixture takes on a reddish color. Taste for salt. Add cilantro and lemon juice, stir, and remove from heat.

Serve by spooning clear broth into bowls, leaving dhal solids behind.

PREPARATION TIME: 1 HOUR 30 MINUTES   SERVES: 6

Pulisheri Soup

 This buttermilk soup (pictured on page 50) is based on a Kerala curry, pulisheri. *My aunt makes a wonderful version of it, sometimes replacing the cucumber with banana or pineapple. Since it is very thin, my father and I adapted it to be a soup. If possible, use curry leaves to make this one, or it will lack the proper flavor and aroma.*

1 medium cucumber, peeled, seeded, and cut into ½-inch (1½ cm) dice (about 1 cup; 225g)
1 cup (240 ml) water
1 green chili (serrano, Thai, or jalapeño), split lengthwise
¼ teaspoon ground cumin
⅛ teaspoon ground red pepper (cayenne)
¼ teaspoon ground turmeric
1¼ teaspoons salt
2 cups (480 ml) buttermilk

½ teaspoon mustard seeds
⅛ teaspoon fenugreek seeds
10 curry leaves or 3 bay leaves
1 tablespoon vegetable oil

In a 3-quart (3 L) saucepan over medium heat, cook diced cucumber with water, green chili, cumin, red pepper, turmeric, and salt until cucumber is very soft and water becomes syrupy, 10 to 15 minutes. Add buttermilk and heat carefully until buttermilk is almost boiling, but do not allow to boil. Cover and remove from heat.

In a small covered frying pan heat mustard seeds, fenugreek seeds, and curry leaves in oil over medium-high heat, until mustard seeds begin to pop. Add contents of pan to buttermilk mixture. Pour a ladleful of buttermilk mixture into pan to recover remaining seeds and leaves, then pour back into soup. Taste for salt.

Serve warm.

PREPARATION TIME: 30 MINUTES   SERVES: 4

Mulligatawny Soup

Loosely based on **rasam** *(see page 53), this dish was invented to satisfy the British appetite for soup. The name is derived from the Tamil (language of Tamil Nadu) words* **milagu** *and* **tunni**, *which mean "pepper water." Although there are countless versions, meat stock, onion, and spices generally form the soup's base.*

1 cup (240 ml) water

1 cup (240 ml) canned unsweetened
   coconut milk

1½ cups (360 ml) chicken broth

1 cup (225g) chopped tomatoes, fresh or
   canned, drained

1 cup (180g) thinly sliced onion

½ teaspoon minced garlic

2 slices ginger, each ⅛ inch (½ cm) thick

¼ teaspoon fennel seeds, coarsely ground

2 whole cloves

½-inch (1½ cm) piece cinnamon stick

1 to 1½ teaspoons salt

1 green chili (serrano, Thai, or jalapeño),
   split lengthwise

Spice mixture

   ½ teaspoon ground coriander

   ¼ teaspoon ground cumin

   ⅛ teaspoon ground turmeric

   ⅛ teaspoon ground red pepper (cayenne)

½ cup (120 ml) canned unsweetened
   coconut milk

1 tablespoon fresh lime juice

¼ teaspoon mustard seeds

1 dried red pepper

10 curry leaves or 2 bay leaves

1 tablespoon vegetable oil

In a 3-quart (3 L) saucepan combine water, 1 cup (240 ml) coconut milk, chicken broth, tomatoes, onion, garlic, ginger, fennel seeds, cloves, cinnamon, salt, green chili, and spice mixture. Simmer for about 20 minutes, or until onion and tomato are soft.

Add ½ cup (120 ml) coconut milk and lime juice. Bring barely to a simmer and turn off heat.

In a small covered frying pan over medium-high heat, heat mustard seeds, dried red pepper, and curry leaves in oil until seeds begin to pop. When popping subsides, pour contents of pan over soup and stir.

PREPARATION TIME: 35 MINUTES   SERVES: 4

Tomato and Onion Salad

Make this salad (pictured on page 50) when good ripe tomatoes are available. As a variation, add ½ cup (120 ml) low-fat yogurt with tomatoes, and additional salt as needed.

¼ cup (60 ml) white vinegar
1 teaspoon minced green chili (serrano, Thai, or jalapeño)
¾ teaspoon salt
1 cup (180g) thinly sliced onion

4 large ripe tomatoes, cut into thin wedges like orange segments (about 4 cups; 900g)

In a medium bowl combine vinegar, green chili, and salt. Toss with onion, and set aside for 5 minutes to mellow onion.

Add tomato and combine thoroughly. Set aside for 15 minutes before serving.

PREPARATION TIME: 25 MINUTES, INCLUDING 15 MINUTES STANDING TIME   SERVES: 6 TO 8

Tomato and Cucumber Salad

This zesty salad (pictured on page 133) is somewhat like a thick salsa. It makes a nice companion to dry meat dishes like Lamb-Fry (page 132) or Chicken Tikka (page 121), but it could fit into any menu.

2 large ripe tomatoes, seeded and coarsely chopped (about 2 cups; 450g)
1 medium cucumber, peeled, seeded, and coarsely chopped (about 1 cup; 225g)
1 to 2 teaspoons minced green chili (serrano, Thai, or jalapeño), adjusted to taste
1 tablespoon fresh lemon juice
¼ cup (15g) chopped cilantro (fresh coriander)

¼ teaspoon salt
Cilantro (fresh coriander) sprigs

In a medium bowl combine tomatoes, cucumber, green chili, lemon juice, and cilantro; set aside.

Add salt just prior to serving and garnish with sprigs of fresh coriander.

PREPARATION TIME: 10 MINUTES   SERVES: 6 TO 8

Raita

 This yogurt and cucumber salad is a North Indian favorite, perhaps because it provides such a contrast to the intense flavors of the curries. The green chili is optional if you want it to be mild.

2 medium cucumbers, peeled, seeded,
  and coarsely grated or finely chopped
  (about 2 cups; 450g)
1 cup (180g) minced white onion
½ teaspoon minced green chili (serrano,
  Thai, or jalapeño; optional)
2 cups (480 ml) plain low-fat yogurt
½ teaspoon ground cumin
¹⁄₁₆ teaspoon ground red pepper (cayenne)
¹⁄₁₆ teaspoon ground black pepper
1 teaspoon salt

In a medium bowl combine all ingredients. Set aside for 20 minutes before serving; consistency of raita should be slightly runnier than yogurt. Taste for salt.

Serve cool or at room temperature.

PREPARATION TIME: 30 MINUTES,
INCLUDING STANDING TIME
YIELD: ABOUT 4 CUPS (960 ML)

SERVES: 8

Ginger Yogurt

 A zesty Kerala side dish with a nice ginger bite. This one benefits from sitting before serving.

2 cups (480 ml) plain low-fat yogurt
1 tablespoon grated ginger
½ teaspoon minced green chili (serrano,
  Thai, or jalapeño)
½ to 1 teaspoon salt, as needed to balance
  other flavors

In a small bowl combine all ingredients. Let stand for 1 hour before serving. Taste for salt.

PREPARATION TIME: 10 MINUTES,
PLUS 1 HOUR STANDING TIME
YIELD: ABOUT 2 CUPS (480 ML)

SERVES: 8

Coconut Chutney

 This thick and flavorful chutney (pictured on page 26) accompanies virtually every South Indian snack. Serve it with Split Pea Vada (page 38), Potato Vada (page 40), Bonda (page 42), Rava Idli (page 30), and Rava Dosa (page 32). It has the best flavor when made with fresh curry leaves. Since it doesn't keep well in the refrigerator, plan on making and eating it the same day.

1 cup (115g) grated unsweetened coconut
½ cup (85g) finely chopped onion
1 teaspoon minced ginger
1 teaspoon minced green chili (serrano,
    Thai, or jalapeño)
¼ cup (60 ml) plain low-fat yogurt
½ teaspoon fresh lemon juice
¾ teaspoon salt
½ (120 ml) cup water, as needed

½ teaspoon mustard seeds
2 dried red peppers
8 curry leaves or 2 bay leaves
2 tablespoons vegetable oil

In a food processor or blender grind coconut, onion, ginger, green chili, yogurt, lemon juice, and salt with as little water as needed for a moderately thick (not watery) consistency. Set aside.

In a covered medium frying pan heat mustard seeds, dried red peppers, and curry leaves in oil over medium-high heat until the seeds begin to pop. Uncover, add ground coconut mixture, and stir for 10 seconds. Remove from heat and transfer to serving bowl.

Serve at room temperature as dip for snacks.

PREPARATION TIME: 20 MINUTES   SERVES: 8
YIELD: ABOUT 1½ CUPS (360 ML)

Tamarind Chutney

 A very popular tart and sweet chutney (pictured on page 50) that tastes great with Samosas (page 46) or Pakora (page 41). Tamarind pulp is required for this recipe because its flavor is much fruitier than tamarind concentrate. The fibrous pulp is boiled with water, and the strained juice is used to make the chutney. The pulp is sold in a soft block in Indian grocery stores.

¼ cup (60g) tamarind pulp (not concentrate)
1 cup (240 ml) water

¼ teaspoon cumin seeds

¼ cup (50g) dark brown sugar (packed)
4 slices ginger, each ⅛ inch (½ cm) thick
¼ teaspoon salt

⅛ teaspoon Garam Masala (page 171)

In a 1-quart (1 L) saucepan combine tamarind pulp and water and boil together for 1 minute, stirring to break up tamarind. Set aside for 15 minutes.

Meanwhile, in a small frying pan over medium heat, dry-roast cumin seeds until they brown and release their fragrance. Remove from heat and grind with a mortar and pestle. Set aside.

Strain tamarind pulp through a sieve into a bowl, pressing out all liquid. Discard pulp and return juice to the saucepan. Add ground cumin, brown sugar, ginger, and salt and bring to a boil. Turn down heat and simmer until mixture becomes a thin syrup (it will thicken as it cools).

Remove from heat, stir in garam masala, and remove ginger slices.

Serve at room temperature.

Note: Refrigerated, dip will keep for 2 weeks.

PREPARATION TIME: 30 MINUTES   SERVES: 12
YIELD: ABOUT 1 CUP (240 ML)

Cilantro and Mint Chutney

 Everyone seems to love this chutney. It makes an ideal companion to fried snacks like Pakora (page 41), Baji (page 43), and Samosas (page 46). This version (pictured on page 50) is somewhat spicy, so reduce the green chili if you want it less hot.

2 cups (120g) cilantro (fresh coriander)
    leaves and tender stems (loosely packed)
1 cup (60g) mint leaves (loosely packed)
1 cup (180g) chopped onion
½ teaspoon minced garlic
½ teaspoon minced ginger
½ teaspoon ground cumin
1 teaspoon minced green chili (serrano,
    Thai, or jalapeño)
½ teaspoon sugar
½ teaspoon salt
2 tablespoons fresh lemon juice
3 tablespoons plain low-fat yogurt,
    or as needed

In a food processor or blender combine all ingredients and process to a smooth purée, adding more or less yogurt as needed to obtain a creamy (not watery) consistency.

Note: Refrigerated in an airtight container, this chutney keeps up to 1 week.

PREPARATION TIME: 10 MINUTES   SERVES: 8 TO 12
YIELD: ABOUT 1 CUP (240 ML)

Bunches of fresh cilantro for sale with ginger, scallions, and green chilies

Spicy Tomato Chutney

Red pepper gives this chutney a serious kick. It goes particularly well with the strong flavors of meaty snacks like Meat Cutlets (page 44) and Shami Kabab (page 45).

½ teaspoon mustard seeds
¼ teaspoon cumin seeds
1 tablespoon vegetable oil

½ teaspoon minced garlic
½ teaspoon minced ginger
2 cups (450g) finely chopped seeded fresh
    tomatoes
½ teaspoon ground red pepper (cayenne)
⅛ teaspoon ground turmeric
1 teaspoon salt
1 teaspoon fresh lemon juice

In a covered medium frying pan heat mustard and cumin seeds in oil over medium-high heat. When mustard seeds begin to pop, turn heat down to medium.

Add garlic and ginger; stir for 30 seconds. Add tomato and simmer for 2 to 3 minutes. Add red pepper, turmeric, and salt and fry until tomatoes are well cooked and broken up. Stir frequently to prevent sticking. Add lemon juice and remove from heat.

PREPARATION TIME: 15 MINUTES   SERVES: 8 TO 12
YIELD: ABOUT 1½ CUPS (360 ML)

Chutney for Kabab

Designed to accompany Shami Kabab (page 45), this chutney also complements Lamb Kabab (page 134). It resembles salsa in its consistency.

2 cups (450g) chopped seeded fresh tomatoes
2 teaspoons minced garlic
1 teaspoon minced green chili (serrano,
    Thai, or jalapeño)
¼ cup (15g) cilantro (fresh coriander) leaves
    (loosely packed)
4 teaspoons fresh lemon juice
¼ teaspoon salt

In a food processor or blender combine tomatoes, garlic, green chili, cilantro, lemon juice, and salt. If using a food processor, pulse 10 to 12 times; if using a blender, process briefly on a low setting. Do not purée.

PREPARATION TIME: 10 MINUTES   SERVES: 8
YIELD: ABOUT 1½ CUPS (360 ML)

Dhals and Vegetables

A RICH VARIETY of legumes (*dhal*) and vegetables has made vegetarianism possible in India for nearly two thousand years. This chapter explores typical *dhal* and vegetable dishes from Kerala, as well as many other classic favorites, using ingredients widely available outside India. ▣ *DHAL*—THE PRIMARY source of protein in a vegetarian diet—is served in one form or another at nearly every meal. For breakfast, *idli* or *dosa* are eaten with Sambar (page 68), a hot, soupy mixture of legumes and vegetables. At a large South Indian meal, curries are eaten alongside a mixture of *dhal* cooked with spices, rice, and *ghee* (clarified butter). Indian grocery stores sell many varieties of raw *dhal*, but the flat, golden *thoor dhal* is preferred for most of the recipes in this chapter. Regular yellow split peas (sold in supermarkets) can be substituted. ▣ WHEN COOKING *thoor dhal*, simmer the legumes in water until quite soft. Never add salt or acidic ingredients like lemon juice at this stage because they prevent the legumes from softening. You can reduce the initial cooking time by approximately 15 minutes by soaking the peas for a few hours before simmering. ▣ KERALA NAYAR wedding feasts always feature the same complement of curries that epitomize classic vegetarian cooking of the region. A typical feast would begin with *dhal*, *ghee*, and rice, followed by *sambar* and rice. Accompanying these courses are *aviyal* (mixed vegetables cooked with a grated-coconut and tamarind sauce), *thoren* (a shredded vegetable stir-fried with coconut), *kichadi* (a chopped

Front to back: Sweet Potato Erisheri, Green Beans Thoren, Potatoes and Cauliflower with Peas

63

vegetable with coconut and yogurt), *pachadi* (a chopped vegetable in a yogurt sauce), and *pappadam*. All of these simple and versatile recipes can be made with nearly any seasonal or regional vegetables.

Erisheri, composed of cubed squash (or sweet potato; page 72) and toasted coconut, is another Kerala standard. It's a fairly thick curry, as is *kootu,* a dish made with legumes cooked with vegetables. The Potatoes and Onions (page 86) can be enjoyed as part of a large meal or as a stuffing for the wheat crepes, Rava Dosa (page 32). Thickened with coconut milk, the somewhat richer Potatoes and Onions with Tomatoes (page 88) makes an ideal accompaniment for the rice pancakes, Appam (page 34), as does the soupy, ginger-flavored coconut milk curry called Potato Stew (page 87). The coconut milk in these dishes marks them as typical South Indian fare.

From the north come some of India's best-known vegetable dishes, like Potato Korma (page 92) —a vegetable version of the famous creamy Lamb Korma—and Eggplant Bhurta (page 96), made from chopped roasted eggplant (aubergine). Curried eggplant, or *brinjal* as the vegetable was called,

quickly became a favorite of the British. The robust preparation of Eggplant and Tomatoes (page 95) is a family favorite. *Paneer,* a North Indian specialty of cubed, lightly fried homemade cheese, is combined with peas and spinach in two popular curries. Cholé (page 93), a North Indian dish from Punjab, is a fragrant curry made with chickpeas and tomatoes and is often eaten with Puri (page 152) as a light snack.

Stir-frying vegetables in a wok-shaped vessel is practiced throughout India. Using a few simple seasonings like mustard seeds, cumin seeds, and green chili, this quick, dry method is well suited to vegetables like peas, okra, and broccoli. Since potatoes take longer to cook, it is best to either cube and boil them first, as in Potatoes and Bell Peppers (page 90), or gently steam them, as in Potatoes and Cauliflower with Peas (page 91).

The spectrum of Indian vegetable curries varies greatly in terms of texture, color, and complexity. When putting together a menu, try to select the dishes with care to ensure an interesting range for the eyes as well as the palate.

Dhal with Coconut

 A wide variety of Indian legumes can be used to make dhal, *but most cooks prefer* thoor dhal, *a thin yellow split legume sold in Indian grocery stores. This Kerala-inspired recipe features coconut, mustard seeds, and lemon juice.*

¼ teaspoon mustard seeds
2 tablespoons vegetable oil
¼ cup (45g) chopped onion
1 teaspoon minced garlic
Spice mixture
    ½ teaspoon ground cumin
    ⅛ teaspoon ground red pepper (cayenne)
    ⅛ teaspoon ground turmeric

1 cup (180g) thoor dhal or yellow split peas
2½ cups (600 ml) water

¼ cup (30g) grated unsweetened coconut
1 teaspoon salt

2 teaspoons fresh lemon juice
2 teaspoons Ghee (page 172)

In a small covered frying pan heat mustard seeds over medium-high heat in oil until seeds begin to pop; uncover, add onion, and fry until edges are nicely browned. Add garlic and spice mixture and fry for 20 seconds, stirring constantly. Remove from heat and set aside.

In a 3-quart (3 L) saucepan bring thoor dhal (or split peas) and water to a boil; turn heat down and add onion mixture to simmering dhal. Cover and continue simmering for 30 minutes (45 minutes for split peas), watching for spilling. (Remove cover to let bubbles subside if spilling occurs.) The peas will hold their shape even as the water level drops, but will break under the slightest pressure when cooked.

Mash dhal with a potato masher or back of a spoon 6 to 8 times, to break up roughly. Stir in the coconut and salt. Partially cover and simmer for 5 to 10 minutes, adding a small amount of water if mixture gets too thick. Check often to make sure peas are not sticking to the bottom. Mixture should be the consistency of thick soup.

Stir in lemon juice. Remove from heat and stir in ghee.

PREPARATION TIME: 1 HOUR TO 1 HOUR 15 MINUTES
SERVES: 8

Spicy Dhal with Tomatoes

 This recipe comes from our friend Vanaja from the eastern state of Andhra Pradesh—famous for its fiery food. We always enjoy her cooking, but we especially love eating her dhal, *colorful with tomatoes and cilantro and zesty with green chili. Adjust the number of chilies to suit your taste.*

1 cup (180g) thoor dhal or yellow split peas
2½ cups (600 ml) water
¼ teaspoon ground turmeric

¼ teaspoon cumin seeds
¼ teaspoon mustard seeds
¼ teaspoon crushed red pepper
2 tablespoons vegetable oil
1 cup (180g) chopped onion
1 teaspoon minced garlic
2 to 3 green chilies (serrano, Thai, or
　jalapeño), split lengthwise

1 cup (225g) chopped tomatoes,
　fresh or canned, drained

1 teaspoon salt

2 tablespoons chopped cilantro
　(fresh coriander)

In a medium saucepan bring thoor dhal (or yellow split peas), water, and turmeric to a boil; turn heat down, cover, and let simmer 30 minutes (45 minutes for split peas), watching for spilling. (Remove cover to let bubbles subside if spilling occurs.)

While dhal cooks over medium-high heat, in heavy 3-quart (3 L) covered saucepan, heat cumin seeds, mustard seeds, and crushed red pepper in oil until mustard seeds begin to pop. Turn heat down to medium, add onion, garlic, and green chilies, and fry for about 5 minutes until onion is soft.

Add the tomatoes and cook, stirring, until they are soft. Do not overcook; tomato pieces should hold their shape.

When dhal is cooked and completely tender, mash with a potato masher or back of a spoon 6 to 8 times, to break up roughly. Add to tomato and spice mixture, stir in salt, and bring to a boil. Simmer for 2 minutes, adding more water if necessary for a pourable consistency. Taste for salt.

Remove from heat and garnish with chopped cilantro.

PREPARATION TIME: 45 MINUTES TO 1 HOUR 15 MINUTES
SERVES: 6 TO 8

Spinach Dhal

 Many Indian households serve dhal *daily, and every cook has a method for cooking and seasoning this staple. This one (pictured on page 89) belonged to my grandmother. If you don't have green split peas on hand, substitute yellow, but green gives the dish a nice color.*

1 cup (180g) green or yellow split peas
2½ cups (600 ml) water

One-third 10-ounce (285g) package frozen
    chopped spinach, thawed and partially
    drained, or 2 cups (85g) finely chopped
    fresh spinach (packed)
½ cup (60g) grated unsweetened coconut
1 teaspoon minced garlic
2 teaspoons ground cumin
⅛ teaspoon ground red pepper (cayenne)
¾ teaspoon salt
½ cup (120 ml) water, or as needed

½ teaspoon mustard seeds
2 dried red peppers
10 curry leaves or 2 bay leaves
1 tablespoon vegetable oil

In a 3-quart (3 L) saucepan bring split peas and 2½ cups (600 ml) water to a boil; turn heat down, cover, and let simmer for 45 minutes, watching for spilling. (Remove cover to let bubbles subside if spilling occurs.)

When peas are cooked and completely tender, mash with potato masher or back of spoon 6 to 8 times, to break up roughly. Add chopped spinach. As mixture begins to simmer again, add coconut, garlic, ground cumin, ground red pepper, and salt, and continue to simmer for another 20 minutes. Add ½ cup water (120 ml) or more if necessary to maintain consistency of moderately thick soup. Remove from heat.

In a small covered frying pan heat mustard seeds, dried red peppers, and curry leaves in oil over medium-high heat until mustard seeds begin to pop. Pour contents of skillet over cooked peas and stir. Taste for salt.

PREPARATION TIME: 1 HOUR 15 MINUTES   SERVES: 6 TO 8

Sambar

This is a spicy stew of legumes and vegetables (pictured on page 26), and in the southern state of Tamil Nadu, no meal is complete without it. It is essential that the fenugreek, asafetida, and tamarind (available in Indian and Asian markets) are used, because they provide the distinctive tangy quality. Serve with Coconut Chutney (page 58), to accompany Rava Idli (page 30) or Rava Dosa (page 32), or in place of dhal *with a full meal.*

½ cup (90g) thoor dhal or yellow split peas
1¼ cups (300 ml) water
⅛ teaspoon ground turmeric

¼ teaspoon tamarind concentrate
1 tablespoon hot water

¼ teaspoon mustard seeds
¼ teaspoon fenugreek seeds
⅛ teaspoon ground asafetida
1 tablespoon vegetable oil

2 cups (480 ml) water
1½ teaspoons salt
1 tablespoon Sambar Spice Blend (page 170)
1 large boiling potato, peeled and cut into
    ¾-inch (2 cm) cubes (about 1½ cups;
    255g)
1 cup (225g) coarsely chopped fresh tomatoes
1 cup (180g) coarsely chopped onion
⅓ cup (60g) cut green beans (1-inch
    [2½ cm] lengths)
1 green chili (serrano, Thai, or jalapeño),
    split lengthwise
5 to 6 sprigs cilantro (fresh coriander)
10 curry leaves or 2 bay leaves

In a small saucepan combine thoor dhal or split peas, 1¼ cups (300 ml) water, and turmeric and bring to a boil. Turn heat down to low and simmer, covered, for 30 minutes or until very soft (45 minutes for split peas).

While dhal cooks, dissolve tamarind concentrate in 1 tablespoon hot water; set aside.

In a 3-quart (3 L) covered saucepan over medium-high heat, heat mustard seeds, fenugreek seeds, and asafetida in oil until mustard seeds begin to pop.

After the seeds have popped for a few moments, add 2 cups (480 ml) water, salt, spice blend, dissolved tamarind, potato, tomatoes, onion, green beans, green chili, cilantro, and curry leaves and simmer over medium-low heat until the potatoes are tender (about 20 minutes).

When dhal is cooked and completely tender, mash with a potato masher or back of a spoon 6 to 8 times, to break up roughly. Stir into cooked vegetable and spice mixture in saucepan and simmer for another 10 minutes. Add more water if necessary to attain a soupy consistency.

PREPARATION TIME: 1 HOUR   SERVES: 8

Kootu

 Kootu *(pronounced KOO-teh), a widely enjoyed vegetable preparation from Tamil Nadu, incorporates legumes and coconut into a thick, protein-rich curry. Served in place of* dhal, *this potato and cabbage curry makes a nice addition to a menu of Chicken Vindaloo (page 118), Stir-Fried Okra (page 78), Pullao with Peas (page 149), and Ginger Yogurt (page 57).*

½ cup (90g) thoor dhal or yellow split peas
⅛ teaspoon ground turmeric
1½ cups (360 ml) water

1 cup (180g) coarsely grated or chopped
    cabbage
1 medium boiling potato, peeled and cut into
    ½-inch dice (about 1 cup; 170g)
¼ cup (30g) grated unsweetened coconut,
    ground finer in a small food processor
    or blender
1 green chili (serrano, Thai, or jalapeño),
    split lengthwise
Spice mixture
    ½ teaspoon ground coriander
    ⅛ teaspoon ground red pepper (cayenne)
    ⅛ teaspoon ground black pepper
1 teaspoon salt
1½ cups (360 ml) water

¼ teaspoon mustard seeds
¼ teaspoon cumin seeds
10 curry leaves or 2 bay leaves
1 tablespoon vegetable oil

In a 3-quart (3 L) saucepan bring thoor dhal or split peas, turmeric, and 1½ cups (360 ml) water to boil; turn heat down to low and simmer, covered, for 30 minutes (45 minutes for split peas).

Meanwhile, in a second saucepan combine cabbage, potato, coconut, green chili, spice mixture, salt, and 1½ cups (360 ml) water. Cook, covered, until potatoes are tender, about 15 minutes. Remove from heat.

When dhal is cooked and completely tender, mash with potato masher or back of a spoon 6 to 8 times, to break up roughly. Stir in potato mixture and simmer for 10 minutes longer. If mixture is too thick, add more water; consistency should be slightly thin.

In a small covered frying pan over medium-high heat, heat mustard seeds, cumin seeds, and curry leaves in oil until mustard seeds begin to pop. Pour contents of pan over dhal and vegetables and stir to combine. Taste for salt.

PREPARATION TIME: 50 MINUTES   SERVES: 4 TO 6

Aviyal

 Aviyal *(pronounced ah-VEAL), a Kerala standard (pictured on page 98), combines coconut and tamarind with a range of vegetables, including green bananas and gourds. We make it with a number of vegetables that are widely available, but feel free to make substitutions. In Malayalam (Kerala's language) the name of this curry has come to mean "mixed bag" because of its many ingredients.*

¼ teaspoon tamarind concentrate

2 tablespoons hot water

1 medium boiling potato, peeled and cut into
finger-width pieces 2 inches (5 cm) long
(about 1 cup; 180g)

1 medium carrot, peeled, and cut same as
potato (about 1 cup; 170g)

1 green chili (serrano, Thai, or jalapeño),
split lengthwise

1 teaspoon salt

⅛ teaspoon ground red pepper (cayenne)

⅛ teaspoon ground turmeric

1½ cups (360 ml) water

1 medium cucumber, peeled, seeded, and cut
same as potato (about 1 cup; 225g)

1 cup (140g) cut green beans (1- to 1½-inch
[2½ to 4 cm] lengths)

½ cup (70g) frozen peas

1 cup (115g) grated unsweetened coconut

¼ cup (45g) coarsely chopped onion

1 teaspoon ground cumin

⅛ teaspoon ground red pepper (cayenne)

⅛ teaspoon ground turmeric

1 cup (240 ml) water

20 fresh curry leaves or 4 bay leaves

1 tablespoon vegetable oil

In a small bowl dissolve tamarind concentrate in hot water and set aside.

In a deep pot combine potato and carrot with green chili, salt, red pepper, turmeric, and 1½ cups (360 ml) water and bring to a boil. Boil vegetables for 5 minutes. Add cucumber, beans, peas, and dissolved tamarind and boil for 1 more minute.

While vegetables are boiling, in a food processor or blender combine coconut, onion, cumin, red pepper, turmeric, and remaining 1 cup (240 ml) water and process to a medium-fine consistency (processing in a blender will require more water).

Add coconut mixture to vegetables in pot, turn heat down to medium, and simmer until the vegetables are completely cooked, adding more water if mixture gets too thick to simmer. Add curry leaves or bay leaves and oil. Simmer for another minute and remove from heat.

PREPARATION TIME: 40 MINUTES   SERVES: 6 TO 8

*Basket containing some
ingredients found in aviyal*

Sweet Potato Erisheri

 In Kerala this dish (pictured on page 62) is made with yam or pumpkin, but sweet potato or butternut squash are equally flavorful and easily available. Toasted coconut gives this erisheri *a rich and sweet aroma.*

3 medium sweet potatoes, 2 medium yams, or
    1 small butternut squash, peeled and cut
    into 1-inch cubes (about 4 cups; 680g)
1½ cups (360 ml) water
¼ teaspoon ground turmeric
⅛ teaspoon ground red pepper (cayenne)
1¼ teaspoons salt

¼ cup (30g) grated unsweetened coconut

½ cup drained (115g) canned pinto beans,
    rinsed
¼ cup (30g) grated unsweetened coconut
½ teaspoon minced garlic
¼ teaspoon ground cumin
1 green chili (serrano, Thai, or jalapeño),
    split lengthwise

½ teaspoon mustard seeds
2 dried red peppers
10 curry leaves or 2 bay leaves
2 tablespoons vegetable oil

In a 3-quart (3 L) saucepan combine cubed sweet potatoes, yams, or squash, water, turmeric, red pepper, and salt and bring to a boil. Turn heat down and simmer, covered, 8 to 10 minutes or until tender.

While vegetable is cooking, toast ¼ cup (30g) coconut in a small frying pan over medium heat, stirring continually until it turns a light reddish-brown color and all the white has disappeared. At this point you should smell the coconut aroma; do not let coconut burn! Remove from heat and set aside.

When vegetable is soft, break up with a potato masher or back of a spoon so that some chunks remain. Add toasted coconut, pinto beans, ¼ cup (30g) coconut (untoasted), garlic, cumin, and green chili. Stir briefly and continue cooking for 5 minutes over medium heat. Add water if mixture gets very thick. Set aside.

In a small covered frying pan over medium-high heat, heat mustard seeds, dried red peppers, and curry leaves in oil until mustard seeds begin to pop; stir into vegetable mixture in saucepan. This curry has a thick sauce.

PREPARATION TIME: 45 MINUTES   SERVES: 6 TO 8

Cabbage Thoren

Cabbage works well in this traditional Kerala curry. The key is to finely shred the vegetables so they cook quickly and evenly. An unusual feature of thoren *is the addition of a little raw rice to the hot oil as it is seasoned with mustard seeds and curry leaves. The rice turns white and puffs slightly, resulting in a pleasant crunchy texture among the vegetables.*

¾ cup (85g) grated unsweetened coconut

1 green chili (serrano, Thai, or jalapeño), split
   lengthwise

2 cloves garlic, peeled and crushed with side
   of knife

Spice mixture
   ½ teaspoon ground cumin
   ¼ teaspoon ground coriander
   ⅛ teaspoon ground red pepper (cayenne)
   ⅛ teaspoon ground turmeric

1 teaspoon salt

¼ to ½ cup (60 to 120 ml) water, as needed

1 teaspoon mustard seeds

2 dried red peppers

10 curry leaves or 2 bay leaves

2 tablespoons vegetable oil

1 tablespoon uncooked long-grain rice

½ large cabbage, cored and finely chopped
   (about 6 cups; 450g)

In a small bowl combine coconut, green chili, crushed garlic, spice mixture, and salt with enough water to make a moist ball; set aside.

In a covered wok or large frying pan over high heat, heat mustard seeds, dried red peppers, and curry leaves in oil. When mustard seeds begin to pop, uncover and add rice. Stir until it turns white, 20 to 30 seconds.

Add the cabbage, turn heat down to medium-high, and stir-fry for 2 to 3 minutes, or until cabbage begins to wilt.

Add coconut-spice mixture and stir frequently until cabbage is cooked (about 10 minutes). If too much liquid accumulates in the wok, increase heat and stir constantly. Taste for salt.

PREPARATION TIME: 30 MINUTES   SERVES: 6

*Long Indian green beans surrounded by bitter gourds,
fresh green chilies, and green bananas*

Green Beans Thoren

 A thoren is a dry Kerala curry made with finely chopped vegetables, grated coconut, mustard seeds, and curry leaves. The coconut is mixed into a paste with spices and water before it's added to the cooking vegetables. Since the vegetables are cut small, the cooking time is relatively short. This dish is pictured on page 62.

2 packages (10 ounces [285g] each) frozen
    green beans, thawed, or 1 pound (450g)
    fresh green beans

¾ cup (85g) grated unsweetened coconut
1 green chili (serrano, Thai, or jalapeño),
    split lengthwise
2 cloves garlic, peeled and crushed with
    side of knife
Spice mixture
    ½ teaspoon ground cumin
    ¼ teaspoon ground coriander
    ⅛ teaspoon ground red pepper (cayenne)
    ⅛ teaspoon ground turmeric
1 teaspoon salt
¼ to ½ cup (60 to 120 ml) water, as needed

1 teaspoon mustard seeds
2 dried red peppers
10 curry leaves or 2 bay leaves
2 tablespoons vegetable oil
1 tablespoon uncooked long-grain rice

Cut beans into ¼-inch (¾ cm) pieces and set aside.

In a small bowl combine coconut, green chili, crushed garlic, spice mixture, and salt with enough water to make a moist ball; set aside.

In a covered wok or large frying pan over high heat, heat mustard seeds, red peppers, and curry leaves in oil. When mustard seeds begin to pop, uncover and add rice. Stir until it turns white, 20 to 30 seconds.

Add beans, turn heat down to medium-high, and stir-fry until beans turn bright green and are nearly tender. If using fresh beans, add 1 to 2 tablespoons water and cover with a lid (fresh beans take longer to cook than frozen).

Add coconut-spice mixture and cook, stirring occasionally, until beans are done, 5 to 10 minutes. Taste for salt.

PREPARATION TIME: 30 MINUTES   SERVES: 6

Peas Thoren

 Although we've never actually been served this thoren *in India, my father and I developed it because it's quick to make (no chopping). The sweetness of peas and coconut is quite appealing, making this one of our most popular dishes.*

¾ cup (85g) grated unsweetened coconut
1 green chili (serrano, Thai, or jalapeño),
   split lengthwise
2 cloves garlic, peeled and crushed with side
   of knife
Spice mixture
   ½ teaspoon ground cumin
   ¼ teaspoon ground coriander
   ⅛ teaspoon ground red pepper (cayenne)
   ⅛ teaspoon ground turmeric
1 teaspoon salt
¼ to ½ cup (60 to 120 ml) water, as needed

1 teaspoon mustard seeds
2 dried red peppers
10 curry leaves or 2 bay leaves
2 tablespoons vegetable oil
1 tablespoon uncooked long-grain rice

2 packages (10 ounces [285g] each) frozen
   peas, thawed

In a small bowl combine coconut, green chili, crushed garlic, spice mixture, and salt with enough water to make a moist ball; set aside.

In a covered wok or large frying pan over high heat, heat mustard seeds, dried red peppers, and curry leaves or bay leaves. When mustard seeds begin to pop, add rice and stir until it turns white, 20 to 30 seconds.

Add peas, turn heat down to medium-high, and stir-fry for 1 minute.

Add coconut-spice mixture and stir frequently until peas are done, about 3 minutes. Avoid overcooking.

PREPARATION TIME: 30 MINUTES   SERVES: 6

Stir-Fried Peas

A simple stir-fry dish with mustard seeds that easily fits into a non-Indian menu.

1 teaspoon mustard seeds

4 dried red peppers

10 curry leaves or 4 bay leaves

2 tablespoons vegetable oil

1 cup (180g) finely chopped onion

1 green chili (serrano, Thai, or jalapeño), split
  lengthwise and crushed

2 packages (10 ounces [285g] each) frozen
  peas, thawed

Spice mixture

  ½ teaspoon ground cumin

  ⅛ teaspoon ground coriander

  ⅛ teaspoon ground red pepper (cayenne)

¾ teaspoon salt

In a covered wok or large frying pan over medium-high heat, heat mustard seeds, red peppers, and curry leaves in oil until mustard seeds begin to pop. Uncover, add onion and green chili, and fry until onion is soft.

Add peas, spice mixture, and salt and fry for 2 minutes on medium-high heat, or until peas are cooked.

PREPARATION TIME: 15 MINUTES   SERVES: 6 TO 8

Vegetable stand in Cochin

Stir-Fried Okra

Okra is widely enjoyed in India, where it is known as "lady's finger." In this recipe (pictured on page 112), to give the okra a nice crisp texture, I suggest you stir-fry it over fairly high heat and don't add salt till the end.

1 teaspoon mustard seeds

4 dried red peppers

10 curry leaves or 4 bay leaves

3 tablespoons vegetable oil

1 cup (180g) finely chopped onion

1 green chili (serrano, Thai, or jalapeño),
   split lengthwise

1 pound (450g) fresh okra, trimmed and
   cut into ⅛-inch (½ cm) slices

Spice mixture

   ½ teaspoon ground cumin

   ⅛ teaspoon ground coriander

   ⅛ teaspoon ground red pepper (cayenne)

1 teaspoon salt

In a covered wok or large frying pan over medium-high heat, heat mustard seeds, red pepper, and curry leaves in oil until mustard seeds begin to pop. Uncover, add onion and green chili, and fry until onion is soft.

Turn heat to high. Add okra and fry, stirring constantly, for 2 minutes. Add spice mixture and continue stir-frying until okra browns lightly around the edges (15 to 20 minutes). When okra is browned, stir in salt.

PREPARATION TIME: 30 MINUTES   SERVES: 6 TO 8

A basket of fresh okra

Stir-Fried Broccoli

 Stir-fry dishes are quick to make and add color and crispness to a meal. Although not a vegetable one finds much of in India, broccoli adapts well to Indian seasonings. In this curry passed along to us from our friend Sikka, the aromatic seasonings are cumin seeds and garlic.

1 medium head broccoli

½ teaspoon cumin seeds
2 tablespoons vegetable oil
2 teaspoons minced garlic
2 cups (360g) coarsely chopped onion
1 green chili (serrano, Thai, or jalapeño), split
    lengthwise and crushed
Spice mixture
    ½ teaspoon ground cumin
    ⅛ teaspoon ground coriander
    ⅛ teaspoon ground red pepper (cayenne)
1½ teaspoons salt
1 tablespoon water, or as needed

Cut broccoli into small florets. Stems can be used as well; remove tough skin and cut stems into thin 1-inch (2½ cm) pieces. All this should come to about 5 cups (480g), loosely packed. Set aside.

In a wok or large frying pan over medium heat, heat cumin seeds in oil. When seeds turn light brown, add garlic, onion, and green chili and fry for a few minutes until onion becomes soft. Stir frequently to prevent garlic from sticking.

Add broccoli, spice mixture, and salt and cook, stirring constantly. When broccoli turns bright green all over, turn heat down to medium-low, add 1 tablespoon water, and cover to steam. Check periodically to see if mixture is getting too dry. If it dries out, add more water 1 tablespoon at a time, stirring broccoli with each addition. When cooked, broccoli should be crisp and green with no excess liquid. Taste for salt.

PREPARATION TIME: 25 MINUTES   SERVES: 6 TO 8

Peas Paneer

*A popular North Indian dish combining peas (*matar *in Hindi) and fried cubes of simply prepared, homemade cheese (*paneer*) in a light tomato sauce. Although the* paneer *requires advance preparation, it is not complicated and always worth the effort. The fried* paneer *can be made the evening before and refrigerated overnight.*

1 recipe Paneer (page 173)

3 tablespoons vegetable oil
1 cup (180g) thinly sliced onion
1 teaspoon minced garlic
1 teaspoon minced ginger
1 cup (225g) chopped tomatoes, fresh or
    canned, drained
½ teaspoon minced green chili (serrano,
    Thai, or jalapeño)
1 teaspoon salt
Spice mixture
    2 teaspoons ground coriander
    2 teaspoons ground cumin
    ¼ teaspoon ground red pepper (cayenne)
    ¼ teaspoon ground black pepper
    ¼ teaspoon ground turmeric
¼ cup (60 ml) water

1 cup (240 ml) water
2 packages (10 ounces [285g] each) frozen
    peas, thawed
¼ teaspoon Garam Masala (page 171)

At least 2 hours before serving, prepare paneer. Set aside.

In a wok or large skillet over medium-high heat, fry onion in oil until edges are nicely browned. Add garlic and ginger and stir for another minute. Add tomatoes, green chili, and salt and fry until tomatoes begin to break up.

Add spice mixture and fry for 1 minute. Add ¼ cup (60 ml) water and continue frying until all tomato pieces have softened and broken up.

Add 1 cup (240 ml) water and paneer and simmer until the sauce becomes thick. Add peas and simmer until peas are cooked and sauce is thick, about 5 minutes. Stir in garam masala and remove from heat. Taste for salt.

PREPARATION TIME: 25 MINUTES,
NOT INCLUDING PREPARATION OF PANEER   SERVES: 8

Spinach Paneer

 This well-known North Indian curry, also called saag paneer, *combines chopped spinach with fried cubes of homemade cheese.* Paneer *is eaten primarily in the north, where milk products are commonly used in cooking.*

1 recipe Paneer (page 173)

2 packages (10 ounces [285g] each) frozen chopped spinach, thawed and chopped finer

1 green chili (serrano, Thai, or jalapeño), split lengthwise

1 teaspoon salt

1 cup (180g) thinly sliced onion
3 tablespoons vegetable oil
1 teaspoon minced garlic
1 teaspoon minced ginger
1 cup (225g) chopped tomatoes, fresh or canned, drained
1 teaspoon salt
Spice mixture
    1 teaspoon ground coriander
    1 teaspoon ground cumin
    ¼ teaspoon ground turmeric
    ⅛ teaspoon ground red pepper (cayenne)
¼ cup (60 ml) water

1 cup (240 ml) water
¼ teaspoon Garam Masala (page 171)

At least 2 hours before serving, prepare paneer. Set aside.

In a 2-quart (2 L) saucepan over medium heat, cook spinach with green chili and 1 teaspoon salt for about 5 minutes, or until spinach is well cooked and soft. Remove from heat and set aside.

In a large frying pan over medium-high heat, fry onion in oil until edges are nicely browned. Add garlic and ginger and stir for another minute. Add tomatoes and 1 teaspoon salt, and fry until tomato pieces begin to break up.

Add the spice mixture and stir for a minute. Add ¼ cup (60 ml) water and continue frying until all tomato pieces have softened and broken up.

Stir in cooked spinach. Add 1 cup (240 ml) water and paneer and simmer until water is absorbed. Stir in garam masala and remove from heat. Taste for salt.

PREPARATION TIME: 30 MINUTES,
NOT INCLUDING PREPARATION OF PANEER   SERVES: 8

Spinach Pachadi

 Pachadi (pronounced PUTCH-ah-dee) is a fundamentally South Indian preparation. The Kerala version of this dish is rather like a lightly cooked salad of vegetables, yogurt, and seasonings. I like this recipe because it's quick and the perfect thing when I need a green vegetable to complete a menu. Finely chop the spinach, or the texture will be too tough.

½ cup (90g) coarsely chopped onion

2 tablespoons vegetable oil

2 packages (10 ounces [285g] each) frozen spinach, thawed, partially drained, and very finely chopped, or 28 ounces (800g) fresh spinach, washed, drained, and finely chopped

1 green chili (serrano, Thai, or jalapeño), split lengthwise

1 teaspoon ground cumin

1 teaspoon salt

2 tablespoons water

1 cup (240 ml) plain low-fat yogurt

1 teaspoon mustard seeds

2 dried red peppers

10 curry leaves or 2 bay leaves

1 tablespoon vegetable oil

In a 3-quart (3 L) saucepan over medium heat, fry onion in 2 tablespoons oil until soft. Add spinach, green chili, cumin, salt, and water and cook until spinach is well cooked and soft, and almost all water has evaporated. Remove from heat; stir in yogurt and set aside.

In a small covered frying pan over medium-high heat, heat mustard seeds, curry leaves, and dried red peppers in 1 tablespoon oil until mustard seeds begin to pop. Stir contents of pan into spinach mixture. Taste for salt.

Serve warm or at room temperature.

PREPARATION TIME: 20 MINUTES   SERVES: 6

Tomato Pachadi

A spoonful or two of this sweet and spicy side dish will perk up any palate. Have it with Chicken-Fry (page 115), Green Beans Thoren (page 75), Potatoes and Onions (page 86), and Yogurt Rice (page 148).

½ teaspoon mustard seeds

2 dried red peppers

10 curry leaves or 4 bay leaves

2 tablespoons vegetable oil

2 cups (450g) coarsely chopped fresh
 tomatoes

½ teaspoon mustard seeds, coarsely ground
 with a mortar and pestle

Spice mixture
 ½ teaspoon ground cumin
 ⅛ teaspoon ground red pepper (cayenne)
 ⅛ teaspoon ground turmeric

1 teaspoon salt

1½ teaspoons sugar

½ cup (120 ml) plain low-fat yogurt

In a covered saucepan over medium-high heat, fry ½ teaspoon mustard seeds, dried red peppers, and curry leaves in oil until seeds begin to pop. Uncover and add tomatoes, coarsely ground mustard seeds, spice mixture, salt, and sugar. Fry until mixture thickens and tomato pieces are soft but not disintegrated.

Remove from heat and stir in yogurt. Serve warm or at room temperature.

PREPARATION TIME: 20 MINUTES   SERVES: 6

Market workers delivering their goods

Cucumber Kichadi

 Kichadi *(pronounced KITCH-ah-dee), not to be confused with the North Indian dish called* kicheri *of boiled rice and legumes, is a tangy Kerala side dish with crushed mustard seeds and lemon juice. Kichadis, like* pachadis, *are saladlike preparations to be served in small amounts along with curries and rice.*

2 large cucumbers, peeled, seeded, and cut into ¼-inch (¾ cm) cubes (about 3 cups; 675g)

¼ cup (60 ml) water, as needed

1 green chili (serrano, Thai, or jalapeño), split lengthwise

1 teaspoon salt

1 cup (115g) grated unsweetened coconut, ground finer in small food processor or blender

½ teaspoon mustard seeds, coarsely ground with a mortar and pestle

½ teaspoon cumin seeds, coarsely ground with a mortar and pestle

1 green chili (serrano, Thai, or jalapeño), split lengthwise

5 curry leaves (optional)

½ to ¾ cup (120 to 180 ml) water, as needed

1 cup (240 ml) plain low-fat yogurt

½ cup (120 ml) water

½ teaspoon salt

½ teaspoon mustard seeds

2 dried red peppers

10 curry leaves or 2 bay leaves

2 tablespoons vegetable oil

1 teaspoon fresh lemon juice

In a 3-quart (3 L) saucepan boil the cucumber with ¼ cup (60 ml) water, 1 green chili, and 1 teaspoon salt until pieces become almost translucent and water has nearly disappeared. Partially mash the cucumber with a potato masher or back of spoon. Set aside.

In a food processor or blender combine coconut, coarsely ground mustard and cumin seeds, 1 green chili, and 5 curry leaves with just enough water (½ to ¾ cup; 120 to 180 ml) to make a fine paste.

Add coconut paste to saucepan with cooked cucumber, followed by yogurt, ½ cup (120 ml) water, and ½ teaspoon salt. Adjust with water to form a thick, pourable mixture. Bring mixture just to simmer (do *not* allow to boil) and remove from heat *immediately* or yogurt will separate.

In a small covered frying pan over medium-high heat, heat mustard seeds, red peppers, and remaining 10 curry leaves in oil until mustard seeds begin to pop. Pour contents of pan over cucumber mixture in saucepan; stir in lemon juice. Taste for salt.

Serve at room temperature.

PREPARATION TIME: 35 MINUTES   SERVES: 6 TO 8

Okra Kichadi

My aunt serves a different version of kichadi *every day. Make this one when fresh okra is in season.*

4 tablespoons vegetable oil

1 pound (450g) fresh okra, trimmed and cut into ⅛-inch (½ cm) slices

1 green chili (serrano, Thai, or jalapeño), split lengthwise

1 teaspoon salt

1 cup (115g) grated unsweetened coconut

½ teaspoon mustard seeds, coarsely ground with a mortar and pestle

½ teaspoon cumin seeds, coarsely ground with a mortar and pestle

1 green chili (serrano, Thai, or jalapeño), split lengthwise and stem removed

5 curry leaves (optional)

½ to ¾ cup (120 to 180 ml) water

1 cup (240 ml) plain low-fat yogurt

½ cup (120 ml) water

½ teaspoon salt

½ teaspoon mustard seeds

2 dried red peppers

8 to 10 curry leaves or 2 bay leaves

1 tablespoon vegetable oil

1 teaspoon fresh lemon juice

In a wok or large frying pan heat 3 tablespoons oil over medium to medium-high heat. Add sliced okra and 1 green chili and stir-fry until okra softens and browns around the edges, 15 to 20 minutes. When okra has browned, stir in 1 teaspoon salt. Remove to a bowl and set aside.

In a food processor or blender combine coconut, coarsely ground mustard and cumin seeds, 1 green chili, and 5 curry leaves with just enough water (½ to ¾ cup; 120 to 180 ml) to make a fine paste.

Wipe clean the wok or frying pan used to fry okra, and in it combine coconut paste, yogurt, ½ cup (120 ml) water, and ½ teaspoon salt. Bring mixture just to a simmer (do *not* allow to boil) and remove from heat *immediately* or yogurt will separate.

In a small covered frying pan over medium-high heat, heat mustard seeds, dried red peppers, and 10 curry leaves until seeds begin to pop. Stir contents of pan into coconut-yogurt mixture.

Stir in fried okra, adding more water if necessary to form a thick but pourable mixture. Stir in lemon juice; taste for salt. Serve at room temperature.

PREPARATION TIME: 40 MINUTES   SERVES: 6 TO 8

Potatoes and Onions

 This versatile South Indian curry can be used to make Rava Masala Dosa (page 33), paired with puri, *or served with other curries like Spinach Dhal (page 67), Tamarind Fish (page 106), Tomato and Cucumber Salad (page 56), and Coconut Rice (page 146) for a delicious meal. As a stuffing for Rava Masala Dosa, break up the potato pieces even smaller to make a thick curry with little gravy.*

½ teaspoon mustard seeds

10 curry leaves or 2 bay leaves

3 tablespoons vegetable oil

2 cups (360g) thinly sliced onion

1 teaspoon minced garlic

1 teaspoon minced ginger

Spice mixture

    1 teaspoon ground cumin

    ½ teaspoon ground coriander

    ⅛ teaspoon ground turmeric

    ⅛ teaspoon ground red pepper (cayenne)

3 medium boiling potatoes, peeled and cut into ¾-inch (2 cm) cubes (about 3 cups; 510g)

2 cups (480 ml) water

1 green chili (serrano, Thai, or jalapeño), split lengthwise

1 teaspoon salt

½ teaspoon fresh lemon juice

In a deep medium frying pan heat mustard seeds and curry leaves, covered, in oil over medium-high heat until mustard seeds pop. Uncover and add onion, garlic, and ginger. Fry until onion is soft but not browned. Add spice mixture and stir for 30 seconds.

Stir in potatoes. Add water, green chili, and salt and simmer, uncovered, over medium heat for about 20 minutes, or until potatoes are tender. Break up potato into smaller pieces and stir to thicken sauce. Add water if mixture gets dry, or simmer longer if mixture is very liquid. Taste for salt.

Add lemon juice and remove from heat.

PREPARATION TIME: 30 MINUTES   SERVES: 4 TO 6

Potato Stew

 Not a stew in the Western sense, this Kerala favorite is easy to make and distinctly different from other potato curries. A South Indian stew is a thick curry with a coconut milk gravy, highly seasoned with ginger, green chili, and curry leaves. Stews are typically served with Appam (page 34).

4 large boiling potatoes, peeled and cut into 1-inch (2½ cm) cubes (about 6 cups; 1,020g)

2 cups (360g) thinly sliced onion

2 to 3 green chilies (serrano, Thai, or jalapeño), split lengthwise

4 slices ginger, ⅛ inch (½ cm) thick

1½ cups (360 ml) water

¼ cup (60 ml) canned unsweetened coconut milk

2 teaspoons salt

¾ cup (180 ml) canned unsweetened coconut milk

1 tablespoon vegetable oil

10 curry leaves or 4 bay leaves

In a 4-quart (4 L) saucepan over medium heat, combine potatoes, onion, green chilies, ginger, water, ¼ cup (60 ml) coconut milk, and salt. Bring to boil over medium heat and cook until potatoes are cooked through. Stir frequently, especially when potatoes become tender, so that some of the potato will break off and thicken the sauce.

Add ¾ cup (180 ml) coconut milk and bring mixture to a boil. Add oil and curry leaves, and stir briefly. Taste for salt. Remove from heat and set aside for 15 minutes before serving.

PREPARATION TIME: 40 MINUTES   SERVES: 6

Small Indian red-colored onions

Potatoes and Onions with Tomatoes

 Our friend Shashi makes this beautiful pink curry (pictured opposite) with a fragrant, creamy sauce. It goes wonderfully with Appam (page 34) but could just as easily be eaten with Rava Dosa (page 32) or as a side dish with rice and other curries.

1 cup (180g) thinly sliced onion

3 tablespoons vegetable oil

1 teaspoon minced garlic

Spice mixture

    5 teaspoons ground coriander

    ¼ teaspoon ground red pepper (cayenne)

    ¼ teaspoon ground black pepper

    ¼ teaspoon ground turmeric

1½ cups (340g) chopped tomatoes, fresh or canned, drained

3 medium boiling potatoes, peeled and cut into ¾-inch (2 cm) cubes (about 3 cups; 510g)

¾ cup (180 ml) water

½ cup (120 ml) canned unsweetened coconut milk

1 teaspoon fennel seeds, coarsely ground with a mortar and pestle

1 teaspoon salt

¼ cup (60 ml) canned unsweetened coconut milk

¼ teaspoon mustard seeds

10 curry leaves or 2 bay leaves

1 dried red pepper

1 tablespoon vegetable oil

In a large frying pan over medium-high heat, fry onion in 2 tablespoons oil until edges are nicely browned. Add garlic and stir for 1 minute. Stir in spice mixture and tomatoes and fry until tomato pieces become soft.

Add potatoes, water, ½ cup (120 ml) coconut milk, fennel seeds, and salt, and bring to a boil. Turn heat down and simmer, partially covered, until potatoes are tender and liquid is reduced, about 20 minutes.

Add ¼ cup (60 ml) coconut milk, bring to a boil, and remove from heat. Consistency should be moderately thick. Taste for salt.

In a small covered frying pan over medium-high heat, heat mustard seeds, curry leaves, and dried red pepper in 1 tablespoon oil until mustard seeds begin to pop. Pour contents of pan into potato curry and stir.

PREPARATION TIME: 45 MINUTES   SERVES: 6 TO 8

*Potatoes and Onions with Tomatoes
over Appam with Spinach Dhal*

Potatoes and Bell Peppers

 This dry curry seasoned with mustard and cumin seeds features yellow split peas for added crunchiness. Break up cubed potatoes with a spatula after they boil, otherwise the chunks will be too large to absorb the spices.

Salt

3 medium boiling potatoes, peeled and cut into 1-inch (2½ cm) cubes (about 3 cups; 510g)

½ teaspoon mustard seeds

¼ teaspoon cumin seeds

2 tablespoons yellow split peas

3 tablespoons vegetable oil

1 cup (180g) chopped onion

1 teaspoon minced garlic

1 teaspoon minced green chili (serrano, Thai, or jalapeño)

Spice mixture

    1 teaspoon ground coriander

    1 teaspoon ground cumin

    ¼ teaspoon ground turmeric

    ⅛ teaspoon ground red pepper (cayenne)

1 large green bell pepper, seeded and cut into ½-inch (1½ cm) squares (about 1½ cups; 225g)

1 teaspoon salt

2 teaspoons fresh lime juice

In a medium saucepan of salted water, boil cubed potatoes until just tender, about 10 minutes. Drain, reserving ¾ cup (180 ml) cooking liquid for later use. With a spatula chop potatoes into irregular ½-inch (1½ cm) pieces. Set aside.

In a covered wok or large frying pan over medium-high heat, fry mustard seeds, cumin seeds, and yellow split peas in oil until mustard seeds begin to pop. Uncover and add onion, garlic, and green chili. Fry, stirring continually, until onion is soft.

Add spice mixture and chopped bell pepper; stir for another minute. Add reserved potato cooking liquid and 1 teaspoon salt and simmer until bell pepper is tender. Add potato and continue stirring until spices have blended well with potatoes and moisture is all absorbed. Stir in lime juice. Taste for salt.

PREPARATION TIME: 30 MINUTES   SERVES: 6

Potatoes and Cauliflower with Peas

 This dry, golden curry (pictured on page 62) has a light touch of fennel. Use as little water as possible to cook the vegetables; otherwise they become soggy. Ideally, the edges of the potato and cauliflower will have a hint of a brown crust on them.

3 tablespoons vegetable oil

2 medium boiling potatoes, peeled and cut into ¾-inch (2 cm) cubes (about 2 cups; 340g)

½ head cauliflower, separated into 1-inch (2½ cm) florets (about 3 cups; 450g)

Spice mixture

    1 teaspoon ground cumin

    ½ teaspoon ground coriander

    ¼ teaspoon ground turmeric

    ⅛ teaspoon ground red pepper (cayenne)

½ teaspoon fennel seeds, coarsely ground with a mortar and pestle

1 teaspoon salt

2 teaspoons water, or more as needed

⅔ cup (90g) fresh or frozen peas

1 teaspoon fresh lemon juice

In a wok or nonstick frying pan over medium-high heat, heat oil. Add cubed potatoes and stir briskly for 1 minute. Add cauliflower and stir for another minute.

Stir in the spice mixture, fennel seeds, and salt to mix thoroughly. Add water, turn heat down to medium-low, and cook, covered, until both potatoes and cauliflower are tender, about 8 to 10 minutes, stirring occasionally. If vegetables begin to stick to bottom of wok, add more water in 2-teaspoon increments. Water should not collect in bottom of pan, as this causes vegetables to become soggy.

Uncover and add peas. Turn up heat and stir-fry until potato and cauliflower pieces look dry and peas are cooked (about 2 minutes). Stir in lemon juice and remove from heat. Taste for salt.

PREPARATION TIME: 35 MINUTES   SERVES: 6 TO 8

Potato Korma

 Korma *is a creamy North Indian curry in the elaborate Mughal tradition. In this meatless version, the coriander is roasted in a dry pan to coax out its flavor and enrich the sauce.*

2 cups (360g) thinly sliced onion

3 tablespoons vegetable oil

1 tablespoon unsalted butter

1 teaspoon minced garlic

1 teaspoon minced ginger

1 cup (225g) chopped tomatoes, fresh or
    canned, drained

Spice mixture

    5 teaspoons ground coriander, lightly
        toasted (see note)

    ½ teaspoon ground cumin

    ¼ teaspoon ground red pepper (cayenne)

    ¼ teaspoon ground black pepper

    ¼ teaspoon ground turmeric

    1/16 teaspoon ground cinnamon

    1/16 teaspoon ground cloves

¼ teaspoon fennel seeds, coarsely ground
    with a mortar and pestle

¼ cup (60 ml) water

4 medium boiling potatoes, peeled and cut
    into ¾-inch (2 cm) cubes (about 4 cups;
    680g)

½ cup (120 ml) canned unsweetened
    coconut milk

1½ to 2 teaspoons salt

1½ cups (360 ml) water

3 tablespoons sour cream

In a large heavy frying pan over medium-high heat, fry onion in mixture of oil and butter until it turns light brown. Add garlic, ginger, tomatoes, spice mixture, fennel seeds, and ¼ cup (60 ml) water and continue frying until tomatoes become soft.

Add the potatoes, coconut milk, and salt and stir for another minute. Add 1½ cups (360 ml) water, bring to a boil, and simmer 20 minutes, or until potatoes are nearly tender.

Add sour cream and simmer 10 more minutes until the potatoes are well cooked and sauce becomes thick and creamy. Add more water if mixture gets too dry. Taste for salt.

Note: Toast ground coriander by stirring it in a dry frying pan over medium heat until it browns and releases its fragrance, about 3 minutes. Set aside to cool before using.

PREPARATION TIME: 35 MINUTES   SERVES: 6 TO 8

Cholé

This thick chickpea and tomato curry is a Punjabi dish from my cousin Sreelatha. Cholé *(pronounced CHO-LAY) is served with* chappathi *for a simple light lunch, but you can also combine it with any of the curries in this book.*

¼ teaspoon mustard seeds

¼ teaspoon cumin seeds

3 tablespoons vegetable oil

1 cup (180g) thinly sliced onion

2 cups (450g) chopped tomatoes, fresh or
   canned, drained

Spice mixture

   2 teaspoons ground coriander

   1 teaspoon ground cumin

   ¼ teaspoon ground turmeric

   ⅛ teaspoon ground red pepper (cayenne)

   ⅛ teaspoon ground black pepper

1 teaspoon salt

½ cup (120 ml) water

2 cans (15½ ounces [440g] each) chickpeas
   (garbanzos), rinsed and drained

1 cup (240 ml) water

1 teaspoon fresh lemon juice

2 tablespoons finely chopped cilantro
   (fresh coriander)

In a large deep frying pan over medium-high heat, heat mustard and cumin seeds, covered in oil, until mustard seeds begin to pop. Uncover and add onion. Fry until edges are nicely browned. Add tomatoes and fry until the pieces become soft.

Add spice mixture, salt, and ½ cup (120 ml) water. Continue frying, stirring frequently, until tomatoes break apart, 3 to 5 minutes. Add chickpeas and remaining 1 cup (240 ml) water; bring to a boil, turn heat down, and simmer for 5 minutes. Consistency should be moderately thick. If dry, add more water. Taste for salt.

Remove from heat and mash with a potato masher or back of a spoon 6 or 8 times, to break down some, but not all, of chickpeas. Stir in lemon juice and garnish with chopped cilantro.

PREPARATION TIME: 30 MINUTES   SERVES: 6 TO 8

Chickpeas and Mushrooms

 This earthy curry comes from our Punjabi friend, Mira. Chickpeas (or channa*) are a staple of the north, particularly in the state of Punjab, where a light meal could be as simple as this dish served with Puri (page 152). While mushrooms are not a prominent feature of Indian cuisine, they do grow abundantly in the northern Indian states of Punjab and Kashmir. I like using shiitake mushrooms, when available.*

1 cup (180g) finely chopped onion
1 teaspoon minced garlic
3 tablespoons vegetable oil
2 cups (450g) chopped tomatoes, fresh or
   canned, drained
1 teaspoon minced green chili (serrano,
   Thai, or jalapeño; optional)
Spice mixture
   2 teaspoons ground coriander
   1 teaspoon ground cumin
   ¼ teaspoon ground turmeric
   ⅛ teaspoon ground red pepper (cayenne)
   ⅛ teaspoon ground black pepper
   1/16 teaspoon ground cinnamon
   1/16 teaspoon ground cloves

2 cans (15½ ounces [440g] each) chickpeas
   (garbanzos), rinsed and drained
1¼ teaspoons salt
3 cups (250g) coarsely chopped fresh
   mushrooms
½ cup (120 ml) water

2 teaspoons fresh lemon juice
1 tablespoon coarsely chopped cilantro (fresh
   coriander), plus a few sprigs for garnish

In a wok or large frying pan over medium-high heat, fry onion and garlic in oil. When edges of onions are slightly browned, add tomatoes, green chili if using, and spice mixture. Fry until tomatoes turn orange and pieces break apart, 2 to 5 minutes.

Add chickpeas and salt, and stir until entire mixture is hot. Add mushrooms and water. Turn heat down to medium and stir until mushrooms are tender and gravy is thick, about 10 minutes.

Stir in lemon juice and chopped cilantro and remove from heat. Taste for salt. Garnish with sprigs of cilantro.

PREPARATION TIME: 30 MINUTES   SERVES: 6 TO 8

Eggplant and Tomatoes

 Make this dish in the summertime when eggplants (aubergines) and ripe tomatoes are in abundance. This outstanding, flavorful curry consists of slices of fried eggplant folded into a spicy tomato sauce with fennel seeds. Use a nonstick skillet to minimize the amount of oil needed for frying.

4 thin Japanese eggplants (aubergines), cut into ¼-inch (¾ cm) rounds (about 4 cups; 560g) (see note)

Vegetable oil for frying

¼ teaspoon mustard seeds

½ teaspoon fennel seeds

1 tablespoon vegetable oil

2 cups (450g) chopped tomatoes, fresh or canned, drained

2 teaspoons finely minced ginger

2 teaspoons finely minced garlic

Spice mixture

    2 teaspoons ground coriander

    1 teaspoon ground cumin

    ¼ teaspoon ground red pepper (cayenne)

    ¼ teaspoon ground turmeric

1 teaspoon salt

Water, as necessary

In a large nonstick frying pan over medium to medium-high heat, heat 2 to 3 teaspoons oil. Add enough eggplant (aubergine) to cover pan in a single layer. Fry on both sides until golden brown. Remove to paper towels to drain. Repeat with remaining eggplant, adding more oil as needed for each batch to prevent sticking.

In the same pan wiped clean, over medium-high heat, heat mustard and fennel seeds, covered, in 1 tablespoon oil until mustard seeds begin to pop. Uncover and add tomatoes, ginger, garlic, spice mixture, and salt. Continue frying over medium-high heat, stirring frequently, until tomatoes turn orange and pieces break down to form a soft paste, about 5 minutes.

Add reserved eggplant and stir very gently to combine with tomato mixture. Cover and cook over medium-low heat until eggplant is cooked through, adding water in small amounts if mixture becomes too dry. Taste for salt.

Note: Regular (Italian) eggplant, cut into 1½ × 1½ × ¼-inch (4 × 4 × ¾ cm) pieces, may be substituted.

PREPARATION: 40 MINUTES   SERVES: 4 TO 6

Eggplant Bhurta

 In a North Indian kitchen, the eggplant (aubergine) would be slowly roasted over hot coals to give this curry its characteristically deep, smoky flavor. But in the absence of live coals, our friend Sikka showed us the simpler method of cooking eggplant in a very hot oven until soft. It tastes different but good all the same, especially topped with lots of fresh cilantro.

1 large eggplant (aubergine), 8 to 10 inches
   (20 to 25 cm) long
Vegetable oil

¼ teaspoon cumin seeds
3 tablespoons vegetable oil
2 cups (360g) chopped onion
1 teaspoon minced ginger
1 teaspoon minced garlic
1 teaspoon minced green chili (serrano,
   Thai, or jalapeño)

1 cup (225g) coarsely chopped tomatoes,
   fresh or canned, drained
Spice mixture
   ⅛ teaspoon ground red pepper (cayenne)
   ⅛ teaspoon ground black pepper
   ½ teaspoon ground coriander
1½ teaspoons salt

¼ teaspoon Garam Masala (page 171)
2 tablespoons chopped cilantro
   (fresh coriander)

Preheat oven to 450°F (230°C; mark 8).

Rub the eggplant (aubergine) skin lightly with a few drops of oil and pierce in several places with a knife to prevent it from bursting. Put eggplant in pie pan or on cookie sheet and bake in preheated oven for 40 minutes, or until dark brown and it yields readily when pressed with a spoon. Flesh will have shrunk considerably and possibly even have separated from skin.

Submerge eggplant in cold water for a few minutes. When cool enough to handle, peel off skin, which should come off readily if eggplant is cooked enough. Chop flesh into small pieces, and set aside in a colander to drain.

In a wok or large skillet over medium-high heat, fry cumin seeds in 3 tablespoons oil until slightly brown. Add onion and fry until edges are nicely browned. Add ginger, garlic, and green chili and fry for 1 minute, stirring constantly to prevent sticking.

Add tomatoes, spice mixture, salt, and drained eggplant, stirring well. Stir, still over medium-high heat, until eggplant is thoroughly cooked and all liquid has disappeared (see note). Consistency desired is like a lumpy pâté.

Eggplant

Stir in garam masala and remove from heat. Garnish with chopped cilantro.

Note: Keep temperature high enough and stir constantly to prevent eggplant from boiling in its own juices and becoming a paste.

PREPARATION TIME: 1 HOUR   SERVES: 6

Fish and Shrimp

INDIA'S MALABAR COAST—the fertile strip where Kerala's coastline meets the Arabian Sea—brims with fish and shellfish, and the state's internal network of canals and lagoons (sometimes called "the Venice of the East") provides plenty of freshwater fish. ◼ THE PORTUGUESE introduced Chinese cantilevered fishing nets to Kerala in the sixteenth century, and a number of them are still used in the port of Cochin. The nets, which are attached to the shore, fill with fish at high tide. Then, using counterweights, the nets are hauled out of the water, and the fish brought ashore to be auctioned. While these nets are of great interest to tourists, most fish are caught by fishermen in boats. ◼ FOR FRYING Kerala cooks prefer a flat, white-fleshed sea fish called pomfret because of its firm texture. They usually coat the fish pieces with ground coriander and red chili, fry them until crisp, and serve them with curries and rice. Since pomfret is hard to find in the U.S., substitute white-fleshed fish like haddock, cod, or red snapper to make the Kerala Fried Fish on page 103. ◼ LOCALLY GROWN INGREDIENTS like coconut, tamarind, ginger, and curry leaves feature prominently in fish curries. One of Kerala's best-known dishes, Fish Aviyal (page 101), is made with chunks of fish in a thick aromatic sauce of grated coconut and tamarind, finished with a sprinkling of fresh curry leaves. Fish Molee (page 102), another Kerala specialty, consists of pieces of fish cooked in a piquant sauce of coconut milk, green chilies, and vinegar. South Indian cooks like

Front to back: Aviyal, Stir-Fried Shrimp,
Tamarind Fish, Coconut Rice

my aunt prefer to use an earthenware pot called a *chutty* to make *aviyal* or *molee* because it enhances their flavor, but metal or enamel are acceptable if earthenware is unavailable. To avoid breaking up the pieces, never stir a simmering fish curry; tilt and gently swirl the pan to circulate the sauce.

The coastline that stretches from the southern tip of Kerala northward to the former Portuguese colony of Goa is rich in shellfish as well as fish. From Kerala comes an intense dish known as *thiyal,* a dark robust curry made with browned onions, toasted coconut, and tamarind. The addition of shrimp to this blend, as in Shrimp Thiyal (page 111), makes a truly exceptional curry. When buying shrimp, look for extra-large or jumbo; tiger prawns are lovely if available.

Lush, beautiful Goa became a Christian colony under the Portuguese in 1510, and continued under their control for over four hundred years. The region's cuisine changed dramatically, partly due to the New World foods the Portuguese brought like chilies, potatoes, tomatoes, and cashews, and partly due to their penchant for meat. The hot and sour curry known as *vindaloo* was created in Goa, with lots of hot chilies, vinegar, and coconut, and while it was popular to make it with meat, the Shrimp Vindaloo recipe on page 109 shows its ability to enhance shellfish.

Fish Aviyal simmering in an earthenware "chutty"

The Malabar Coast isn't alone in yielding great harvests of seafood. The Bay of Bengal, on India's eastern shore, is also renowned for its abundance of fresh and saltwater fish. The Bengali term for fish is *jal toori,* or "fruit of the sea," and even strict Brahmins, vegetarian anywhere else, adore eating fish in this area. Bengals make fish curries with mustard-seed oil, which has a distinctively bitter taste. Fish with Mustard Seeds (page 105) suggests the flavor of a Bengali curry, although crushed brown mustard seeds are used in place of mustard oil, which can be quite strong if you are unaccustomed to eating it. For most of the fish preparations, fillets 1½ to 2 inches (4 to 5 cm) thick are best, but steaks are acceptable, too.

Fish Aviyal

 One of the most widely enjoyed fish curries in Kerala, aviyal *(pronounced ah-VEAL) combines two of the state's most plentiful products—fish and coconut. This Kerala standard has a thick sauce of tamarind and grated coconut.*

¼ teaspoon tamarind concentrate
2 tablespoons hot water

2 pounds (900g) fish fillets (red snapper, haddock, or cod)

1½ cups (180g) grated unsweetened coconut
¼ cup (45g) chopped onion
Spice mixture
    1 teaspoon ground cumin
    ¼ teaspoon ground coriander
    ¼ teaspoon ground red pepper (cayenne)
    ¼ teaspoon ground turmeric
1½ teaspoons salt
1¼ cups (300 ml) water
½ cup (120 ml) canned unsweetened coconut milk

1 green chili (serrano, Thai, or jalapeño), split lengthwise

10 curry leaves or 4 bay leaves
1 tablespoon coconut or vegetable oil

In a small bowl dissolve tamarind concentrate in hot water and set aside.

Cut fish fillets crosswise into strips 2 inches (5 cm) wide; set aside.

In a food processor or blender, combine coconut, onion, spice mixture, salt, dissolved tamarind, water, and coconut milk and process to a medium-fine consistency (processing in a blender will require more water).

Transfer coconut mixture to a deep frying pan. Add green chili and bring to a simmer over medium heat. Add fish pieces in one layer (not stacked). There should be enough liquid to nearly cover fish. Continue simmering until fish is opaque, about 10 minutes. Swirl pan or stir very gently, if necessary.

Add curry leaves and oil. Simmer for another minute, then remove from heat. Taste for salt.

PREPARATION TIME: 35 MINUTES   SERVES: 8

Fish Molee

 Molee (pronounced MO-lee) is a mild Kerala Christian fish preparation made with coconut milk and vinegar. Kerala cooks never stir their fish curries; instead, they tilt the pan to circulate the sauce without disturbing the fish. If you want to stir this curry or turn the fish over, do so very gently.

1½ pounds (675g) fish fillets (haddock, cod, or salmon)

1 cup (180g) thinly sliced onion
3 tablespoons vegetable oil
2 teaspoons minced garlic
1 teaspoon minced ginger
2 green chilies (serrano, Thai, or jalapeño), split lengthwise
10 curry leaves or 2 bay leaves
Spice mixture
   3 teaspoons ground coriander
   ½ teaspoon ground cumin
   ⅛ teaspoon ground turmeric
   ⅛ teaspoon ground red pepper (cayenne)
   ⅛ teaspoon ground black pepper
3 tablespoons water

½ cup (120 ml) canned unsweetened coconut milk
1 tablespoon white vinegar
1½ to 2 teaspoons salt

¼ cup (60 ml) canned unsweetened coconut milk

Cut fish fillets into 1½ inch (3.8 cm) cubes; set aside.

In a large frying pan over medium-high heat, fry onion in oil until edges are nicely browned. Add garlic, ginger, green chilies, and curry leaves; stir for 1 minute. Add spice mixture and 3 tablespoons water and stir for 1 minute.

Add ½ cup (120 ml) coconut milk, vinegar, and salt and cook for 2 minutes to allow flavors to blend.

Add fish pieces to pan in a single layer (not stacked). Reduce heat to medium-low and simmer until fish pieces are opaque, about 10 minutes. Try not to turn pieces over or they will break up; instead, swirl pan gently every few minutes to move sauce around.

Add ¼ cup (60 ml) coconut milk, swirl pan to distribute, and turn heat up to medium-high. As soon as sauce comes to a boil, remove from heat.

PREPARATION TIME: 45 MINUTES   SERVES: 6

Kerala Fried Fish

 My father's favorite fish dish took us a long time to adapt, but we finally perfected it with this recipe. In Kerala they coat a trout-size fish called pomfret with spices and then deep-fry it to form a spicy, crisp exterior. We found that cornmeal created such a nice crust we didn't need to deep-fry it. The fish doesn't have the reddish-brown color it does in Kerala, but it still has an excellent flavor and uses less oil.

2 tablespoons finely grated onion

Spice mixture

    3 teaspoons ground coriander

    ¾ teaspoon ground red pepper (cayenne)

    ½ teaspoon ground black pepper

1 teaspoon finely grated garlic

1 teaspoon salt

2 tablespoons vegetable oil

2 pounds (900g) thin fish fillets (red snapper, halibut, or cod)

½ cup (60g) cornmeal

½ cup (70g) all-purpose (plain) flour

2 tablespoons vegetable oil

Combine onion, spice mixture, garlic, salt, and 2 tablespoons oil to form a paste. Smear paste over fish fillets, to cover completely. Refrigerate, covered, for 1 hour.

When ready to fry, dredge fish pieces in combination of cornmeal and flour.

In a large nonstick frying pan over medium-high heat, heat 2 tablespoons oil until very hot. Place fish pieces in oil without crowding (fry in two batches if necessary, adding more oil if needed). Fry, turning once, until golden brown and cooked through.

PREPARATION TIME: 30 MINUTES,
PLUS 1 HOUR MARINATING TIME

SERVES: 8

Fish Baked in Coconut Milk

 Here fish fillets are smothered in a rich coconut and tomato sauce and garnished with cilantro. The fish is baked in two stages: first plain and uncovered, then covered with sauce and sealed in foil, to lock in the flavor and moisture.

2 pounds (900g) thick fish fillets or steaks
    (halibut, cod, or salmon)
4 teaspoons fresh lemon juice
2 tablespoons vegetable oil

2 cups (360g) finely chopped onion
¼ cup (60 ml) vegetable oil
2 teaspoons minced garlic
2 teaspoons minced ginger
1 teaspoon minced green chili (serrano,
    Thai, or jalapeño)
1 cup (225g) chopped fresh tomatoes
Spice mixture
    6 teaspoons ground coriander
    1 teaspoon ground cumin
    ¼ teaspoon ground red pepper (cayenne)
    ¼ teaspoon ground black pepper
    ¼ teaspoon ground turmeric
½ teaspoon fennel seeds, coarsely ground
    with a mortar and pestle
1¼ teaspoons salt
½ cup (120 ml) canned unsweetened
    coconut milk

¼ cup (15g) chopped cilantro
    (fresh coriander)

Cut fillets crosswise into strips 2 inches (5 cm) wide. Rub fish with mixture of lemon juice and oil, cover, and refrigerate for 1 hour.

Meanwhile, preheat oven to 350°F (180°C; mark 4).

In medium frying pan over medium-high heat, fry onion in oil until edges are nicely browned. Add garlic, ginger, and green chili and stir over medium heat for 2 minutes. Add tomatoes, spice mixture, fennel seeds, and salt and fry, stirring constantly until tomato pieces break down to form a lumpy paste. Add coconut milk and simmer about 5 minutes until a thick, rich sauce is formed.

Arrange fish in an oiled baking/serving dish large enough to hold fish in a single layer. Bake, uncovered, for 10 minutes in the preheated oven. Pour sauce over fish, cover tightly with aluminum foil, and return to oven for 15 to 20 minutes (depending on thickness of fish) until fish is opaque.

Garnish with chopped cilantro.

PREPARATION TIME: 50 MINUTES,
PLUS 1 HOUR MARINATING TIME   SERVES: 6 TO 8

Fish with Mustard Seeds

 West Bengal in eastern India is a state renowned for fish curries cooked in mustard oil. Even the Brahmins who follow strict vegetarian diets enjoy eating jal toori *("fruit of the sea"). Sharply flavored mustard oil is replaced here with crushed mustard seeds for a slightly less pungent, but still robust, curry.*

2 pounds (900g) fish fillets (cod, halibut)
¼ teaspoon ground red pepper (cayenne)
¼ teaspoon ground turmeric
1 teaspoon salt
2 teaspoons fresh lemon juice
1 tablespoon vegetable oil

1 cup (180g) finely chopped onion
2 tablespoons vegetable oil
2 teaspoons minced garlic
1 teaspoon mustard seeds, coarsely ground
   with a mortar and pestle
1 cup (225g) chopped fresh tomatoes
Spice mixture
   1 teaspoon ground coriander
   1 teaspoon ground cumin
   ¼ teaspoon ground turmeric
   ¼ teaspoon ground red pepper (cayenne)
   ⅛ teaspoon ground cinnamon
   ⅛ teaspoon ground cloves
   ⅛ teaspoon ground cardamom
3 tablespoons chopped cilantro
   (fresh coriander)
1 teaspoon salt

½ cup (120 ml) plain low-fat yogurt

Preheat oven to 350°F (180°C; mark 4).

Cut fish into strips 2 inches (5 cm) wide. Rub on all sides with mixture of red pepper, turmeric, 1 teaspoon salt, and lemon juice. In a nonstick frying pan heat 1 tablespoon oil over medium heat and lightly brown the fish in two batches if necessary, placing skin side down and turning after a minute or two. Remove fish from pan and set aside.

In the same pan wiped clean, over medium heat, fry onion in 2 tablespoons oil until light brown. Add garlic and mustard seeds and stir for 1 minute. Add tomatoes and spice mixture and fry until tomatoes become very soft and break up. Add cilantro and salt and continue stirring until the mixture becomes a paste.

Remove from heat, add yogurt, and stir to blend.

Arrange fish in a single layer in a baking dish. Pour sauce over fish, cover with aluminum foil, and bake in preheated oven for 20 minutes until opaque.

PREPARATION TIME: 50 MINUTES   SERVES: 8

Tamarind Fish

 The fruits of South India—fish, tamarind, and coconut milk—are blended to form this tart but rich curry (pictured on page 98). Since tamarind is a dominant flavor here, I call for the pulp instead of the concentrate because of its superior, fruitier taste. Firm-fleshed fish are best for this as for all fish curries because they don't break apart with gentle stirring.

2 pounds (900g) fish fillets (halibut, cod,
   or salmon)

1½ tablespoons tamarind pulp
   (not concentrate)
½ cup (120 ml) water

¼ teaspoon mustard seeds
⅛ teaspoon fenugreek seeds
1 dried red pepper
5 to 6 curry leaves (optional)
3 tablespoons vegetable oil
1 cup (180g) finely chopped onion
Spice mixture
   3 teaspoons ground coriander
   ½ teaspoon ground cumin
   ⅛ teaspoon ground red pepper (cayenne)
   ⅛ teaspoon ground black pepper
   ⅛ teaspoon ground turmeric
2 slices ginger, each ⅛ inch (½ cm) thick
1 green chili (serrano, Thai, or jalapeño),
   split lengthwise
¼ cup (60 ml) water
1¼ teaspoons salt

½ cup (120 ml) canned unsweetened
   coconut milk
¼ cup (60 ml) water

Cut fish fillets crosswise into strips 2 inches (5 cm) wide; set aside.

Place tamarind pulp and ½ cup water (120 ml) in a 1-quart (1 L) saucepan and boil together for 5 minutes, stirring to break up tamarind. Remove from heat and strain through sieve into a bowl, pressing out all the liquid. Discard pulp. Set thick tamarind liquid aside.

In a large covered frying pan over medium-high heat, fry mustard seeds, fenugreek seeds, dried red pepper, and curry leaves, if using, in oil until mustard seeds begin to pop. Uncover, add onion, and fry until edges of onion are nicely browned.

Turn heat down to medium and add spice mixture, ginger, green chili, and ¼ cup (60 ml) water. Fry for another 2 minutes, stirring constantly. Add reserved tamarind juice and salt and simmer for about 2 minutes.

Add coconut milk and ¼ cup (60 ml) water and stir to combine thoroughly. Add fish pieces to the pan in a single layer (not stacked). Spoon sauce over pieces and continue

The day's catch waiting to be auctioned

simmering until fish is opaque, about 10 minutes, gently turning pieces over, if necessary. Taste for salt.

Fish pieces will be very soft; transfer carefully to a serving dish, pouring remaining sauce over them.

PREPARATION TIME: 45 MINUTES   SERVES: 6 TO 8

Stir-Fried Shrimp

 A quick stir-fried shrimp dish (pictured on page 98) served either as a dry curry or as an hors d'oeuvre with a Cilantro and Mint Chutney (page 60) dipping sauce.

2 pounds (900g) large shrimp

2 teaspoons minced garlic

Spice mixture

    2 teaspoons ground coriander

    1 teaspoon ground cumin

    ½ teaspoon ground red pepper (cayenne)

    ½ teaspoon ground turmeric

¼ cup (60 ml) vegetable oil

1 teaspoon salt

2 teaspoons fresh lemon juice

2 tablespoons finely chopped scallions

Shell and devein shrimp; rub with mixture of garlic and spice mixture. Set aside for 30 minutes.

In wok or large frying pan over medium-high heat, heat oil. Add marinated shrimp and cook, stirring continually, adding salt while stirring, until shrimp are almost entirely opaque. Add lemon juice and continue frying for another 30 seconds or until shrimp are cooked through. Remove from heat. Do not overcook shrimp.

Stir in scallions. Serve hot.

PREPARATION TIME: 20 MINUTES,
PLUS 30 MINUTES MARINATING TIME   SERVES: 6 TO 8

Fishermen near Cochin at dusk

Shrimp Vindaloo

 Spicy vindaloo *is as delicious with shrimp as with pork or chicken. Have this with Green Bean Thoren (page 75), Potatoes and Bell Peppers (page 90), Tomato and Onion Salad (page 56), and plain rice.*

2 pounds (900g) large shrimp

2 cups (360g) thinly sliced onion
¼ cup (60 ml) vegetable oil
2 teaspoons minced garlic
2 teaspoons minced ginger
Spice mixture
    6 teaspoons ground coriander
    1 teaspoon ground cumin
    ½ teaspoon ground red pepper (cayenne)
    ½ teaspoon ground black pepper
    ¼ teaspoon ground turmeric
    ⅛ teaspoon ground cinnamon
    ⅛ teaspoon ground cloves
¼ cup (60 ml) white vinegar
1 cup (225g) chopped tomatoes, fresh or
    canned, drained
½ teaspoon mustard seeds, coarsely ground
    with a mortar and pestle
¼ cup (60 ml) canned unsweetened
    coconut milk
2 to 3 green chilies (serrano, Thai, or
    jalapeño, depending on desired hotness),
    split lengthwise
1½ teaspoons salt
¾ cup (180 ml) water, or more as needed

Shell and devein shrimp; set aside.

In a large frying pan over medium-high heat, fry onion in oil until edges are nicely browned. Add garlic and ginger and stir for 2 minutes until the onion is medium brown.

Add spice mixture, vinegar, tomatoes, mustard seeds, coconut milk, green chilies, and salt and stir for another 2 minutes. Add water and bring to a boil, then turn heat down and simmer for 5 minutes or until sauce is moderately thick (see note).

Add shrimp and simmer, stirring occasionally. Add a little water if mixture begins to dry out. When shrimp are cooked through and become opaque, about 10 minutes, remove from heat. Taste for salt.

Note: Recipe can be prepared ahead of time up to this point; 10 minutes before serving, bring sauce to a boil and continue following directions.

PREPARATION TIME: 1 HOUR   SERVES: 6 TO 8

Shrimp with Coconut Milk

 A Kerala-style shrimp curry with a rich and lively coconut milk sauce. Omit the green chili if you prefer your curry mild.

1½ pounds (675g) large shrimp

2 cups (360g) thinly sliced onion

¼ cup (60 ml) vegetable oil

1 cup (225g) chopped tomatoes, fresh or canned, drained

1 teaspoon minced ginger

1 teaspoon minced garlic

1 teaspoon minced green chili (serrano, Thai, or jalapeño)

Spice mixture

    4 teaspoons ground coriander

    ½ teaspoon ground cumin

    ½ teaspoon ground red pepper (cayenne)

    ¼ teaspoon ground black pepper

    ¼ teaspoon ground turmeric

    ⅛ teaspoon ground cinnamon

    ⅛ teaspoon ground cloves

½ teaspoon fennel seeds, coarsely ground with a mortar and pestle

1¼ teaspoons salt

½ cup (120 ml) water

¾ cup (180 ml) canned unsweetened coconut milk

½ cup (120 ml) water, or more as needed

Shell and devein shrimp; set aside.

In a deep frying pan over medium-high heat, fry onion in oil until edges are nicely browned. Add tomatoes, garlic, ginger, green chili, spice mixture, fennel seeds, salt, and ½ cup (120 ml) water and fry 5 to 10 minutes, or until tomato pieces become very soft and broken up.

Stir in shrimp, cooking for a minute or two. Add coconut milk and ½ cup (120 ml) water, and bring to boil. There should be enough liquid to nearly cover the shrimp; if not, add water as needed. Turn heat down to medium-low and continue cooking for 10 minutes, or until shrimp are opaque and cooked through. Stir occasionally. Taste for salt.

PREPARATION TIME: 30 MINUTES   SERVES: 6

Shrimp Thiyal

 Thiyal *(pronounced THEEL) is one of my favorite Kerala preparations, made with well-browned onions, toasted coconut, and tamarind for a dark, flavorful sauce.*

2 pounds (900g) large shrimp

½ teaspoon tamarind concentrate
2 tablespoons hot water

½ cup (60g) grated unsweetened coconut, ground finer in a blender or food processor
½ cup (90g) thinly sliced onion
1 tablespoon vegetable oil
Water, as needed

1 cup (180g) sliced onion
2 tablespoons vegetable oil
1 cup (240 ml) water
Spice mixture
    4 teaspoons ground coriander
    ½ teaspoon ground cumin
    ½ teaspoon ground red pepper (cayenne)
    ¼ teaspoon ground turmeric
1 green chili (serrano, Thai, or jalapeño), split lengthwise
1 teaspoon salt

1 teaspoon mustard seeds
10 curry leaves or 4 bay leaves
4 dried red peppers
1 tablespoon vegetable oil

Shell and devein shrimp; set aside.

In a small bowl dissolve tamarind concentrate in hot water and set aside.

In a wok or large frying pan over medium-high heat, toast grated coconut and ½ cup (90g) onion in 1 tablespoon oil, stirring constantly, until the coconut is dark brown. In a food processor or blender process mixture into a fine paste, using as little water as possible. Set aside.

In the same wok or pan, wiped clean, over medium-high heat, fry 1 cup (180g) onion in 2 tablespoons oil until soft. Stir in 1 cup (240 ml) water, spice mixture, green chili, and salt. Turn heat down to medium, add shrimp, and continue cooking for 5 minutes.

Add coconut mixture and tamarind to shrimp and simmer for another 5 minutes, or until shrimp is opaque. Remove from heat.

In a small covered frying pan over medium-high heat, heat mustard seeds, curry leaves, and dried red peppers in 1 tablespoon oil until mustard seeds begin to pop. Pour contents of skillet over shrimp and stir. Taste for salt.

PREPARATION TIME: 40 MINUTES   SERVES: 8

Chicken and Eggs

WHETHER STIR-FRIED, cooked in sauce, or barbecued, chicken responds exceptionally well to Indian seasonings. All over India Muslims, Christians, Sikhs, Parsis, and some Hindus eat chicken. Usually it is cut up and cooked on the bone for added flavor, but many of the recipes in this chapter use boneless pieces for simplicity. ◻ IN THE TROPICAL SOUTH, cooks often put coconut milk in chicken curries to create a thick sauce to soften the spices. My aunt and her daughters made wonderful Kerala-style chicken curries, such as Chicken with Coconut Milk (page 116). From the tradition of Kerala stews comes Chicken Stew with Potatoes (page 117), a white curry made with lots of fresh ginger. This dish is best eaten spooned over hot Appam (page 34), the delicate rice pancakes with thick soft centers. ◻ A VERY DIFFERENT type of Kerala chicken curry is the easy and flavorful Chicken-Fry (page 115). A "fry" is usually a meat or chicken stir-fry, prepared in a wok called a *cheena chutty,* which means "Chinese pot" in Malayalam, the language of Kerala. Without any coconut milk, the liquid is either lemon juice or vinegar, lending the dish a slightly tangy quality. ◻ NORTH INDIAN *tandoori*-style dishes here include Tandoori Chicken (whole pieces; page 120) and Chicken Tikka (boneless cubed meat; page 121), both marinated in spices to tenderize the meat, then cooked in a very hot oven or on a grill. High heat seals in the juices and yields the succulent meat that the *tandoor,* the traditional clay oven, is famous for producing.

Clockwise from top: Stir-Fried Okra, Chappathi,
Chicken Vindaloo, Tandoori Chicken

Many recipes in this chapter call for boneless, skinless chicken thighs, which are flavorful as well as time saving. If you can't find them, just skin and cut up regular thighs, bone in. Remove the skin to allow the spices to penetrate the meat and trim away excess fat to make sure the dish won't be greasy. A shortcut to trimming fat for a wet curry is to let it melt from the chicken in the cooking and then skim it off the top of the finished curry. But don't skim off all the fat or you will lose some of the wonderful flavor.

Eggs are widely enjoyed in India, both as breakfast fare (see pages 36–37) and in curries. Although egg curries are not popular outside of the subcontinent, cooks in both the north and south have created many delicious dishes, often combining halved hard-boiled eggs with spicy tomato sauce; the very tasty Egg Masala (page 122) is the South Indian version with a bit of coconut milk. The other egg curry in this chapter is the classic Kerala dish *aviyal* made with hard-boiled eggs and potatoes in a thick grated-coconut sauce.

Man paddling a long boat through the Kerala backwaters

Chicken-Fry

 Something between a wet and a dry curry, this Kerala original features chunks of chicken with just enough brown sauce to coat. It's extremely quick to prepare. Since it's a stir-fry, I recommend using boneless chicken thighs.

2 pounds (900g) boneless, skinless chicken thighs or about 3 pounds (1,350g) with bone and skin

2 cups (360g) thinly sliced onion

¼ cup (60 ml) vegetable oil

1 teaspoon minced garlic

1 teaspoon minced ginger

1 teaspoon minced green chili (serrano, Thai, or jalapeño)

Spice mixture

    3 teaspoons ground coriander

    ½ teaspoon ground cumin

    ¼ teaspoon ground red pepper (cayenne)

    ¼ teaspoon ground black pepper

    1⁄16 teaspoon ground turmeric

    1⁄16 teaspoon ground cinnamon

    1⁄16 teaspoon ground cloves

2 tablespoons water

1¼ teaspoons salt

½ teaspoon fresh lemon juice

Trim fat from boneless, skinless thighs and cut into 2-inch (5 cm) chunks. If only thighs with bone and skin are available, remove skin and fat and cut thighs into 2 or 3 pieces each, bone in.

In a large nonstick frying pan over medium-high heat, fry onion in oil until edges are nicely browned. Add garlic, ginger, and green chili and stir for 1 minute.

Mix ground spices with water to form a paste. Stir into onion mixture and fry for 1 minute. Add chicken and salt and fry, stirring frequently, until the chicken is cooked through, 10 to 15 minutes. Taste for salt.

Stir in the lemon juice and remove from heat.

PREPARATION TIME: 30 MINUTES   SERVES: 6 TO 8

Chicken with Coconut Milk

 South Indian cooks frequently use coconut milk in meat and chicken curries to thicken the sauces and temper the spices. Fennel seeds, mustard seeds, and curry leaves give this curry a distinctively South Indian flavor.

2 pounds (900g) boneless, skinless chicken
   thighs or about 3 pounds (1,350g) with
   bone and skin
Spice mixture
   6 teaspoons ground coriander
   1 teaspoon ground cumin
   ½ teaspoon ground red pepper (cayenne)
   ½ teaspoon ground black pepper
   ¼ teaspoon ground turmeric
   ⅛ teaspoon ground cinnamon
   ⅛ teaspoon ground cloves

¼ cup (60 ml) vegetable oil
½ teaspoon mustard seeds
10 curry leaves or 2 bay leaves
2 cups (360g) thinly sliced onion
2 teaspoons minced garlic
2 teaspoons minced ginger
1 green chili (serrano, Thai, or jalapeño),
   split lengthwise
½ teaspoon fennel seeds, finely ground with
   a mortar and pestle

1½ teaspoons salt
¼ cup (60 ml) canned unsweetened
   coconut milk
¾ cup (180 ml) water

½ cup (120 ml) canned unsweetened
   coconut milk
1 teaspoon fresh lemon juice

Trim boneless, skinless thighs of fat and cut into 2-inch (5 cm) chunks. If only thighs with bone and skin are available, remove skin and fat and cut thighs into 2 or 3 pieces each, bone in. Rub chicken pieces with mixture of ground spices and refrigerate for 1 hour.

In a covered large frying pan over medium-high heat, heat mustard seeds and curry leaves in oil until mustard seeds begin to pop. Uncover, add onion, and stir until edges are nicely browned. Add garlic, ginger, green chili, and fennel seeds and stir for 2 minutes.

Add chicken pieces and stir for another 3 to 5 minutes, making sure not to burn onion and spices. Add salt, ¼ cup (60 ml) coconut milk, and water. Bring to a boil, turn heat down, and simmer, partially covered, for 30 minutes.

Stir in ½ cup (120 ml) coconut milk and bring to a boil. Add lemon juice and remove from heat. Taste for salt.

PREPARATION TIME: 1 HOUR,
PLUS 1 HOUR MARINATING TIME   SERVES: 6 TO 8

Chicken Stew with Potatoes

 A variation on Lamb Stew with Potatoes (page 129), this South Indian curry is fragrant with coconut milk and curry leaves. Serve it with Appam (page 34) or Rava Dosa (page 32).

2 pounds (900g) boneless skinless chicken thighs or about 3 pounds (1,350g) with bone and skin

2 teaspoons all-purpose flour

3 tablespoons oil

1 cup water (240 ml)
½ cup (120 ml) canned unsweetened coconut milk
1 tablespoon white vinegar
1 teaspoon salt
3 green chilies (serrano, Thai, or jalapeño), split lengthwise
10 curry leaves or 4 bay leaves
1 tablespoon minced ginger

2 tablespoons vegetable oil
1 cup (180g) thinly sliced onion
2-inch (5 cm) piece cinnamon stick
4 whole cloves
⅛ teaspoon peppercorns, slightly crushed with a mortar and pestle

2 medium boiling potatoes, peeled and cut into ¾-inch (2 cm) cubes (about 2 cups; 340g)

½ cup (120 ml) canned unsweetened coconut milk

Trim chicken thighs of fat and cut into 1-inch (2½ cm) cubes. Toss with flour to coat lightly.

In a Dutch oven or flameproof casserole heat oil over medium heat. Add chicken and fry, stirring constantly until all pink color disappears.

Add water, ½ cup (120 ml) coconut milk, vinegar, salt, green chilies, curry leaves, and ginger. Bring to a boil, turn heat down, and simmer, uncovered, for 15 minutes.

While chicken is simmering in a frying pan over medium heat, fry onion in 2 tablespoons oil until soft. Add cinnamon, cloves, and crushed peppercorns; fry 2 minutes or until spices release their fragrance. Do not let onion brown.

When meat has simmered 15 minutes, add onion mixture and cubed potatoes. Bring to a boil, turn heat down, and simmer, covered, for 20 minutes or until potatoes are cooked. (Sauce should be somewhat thick.)

Stir in ½ cup (120 ml) coconut milk. Bring mixture almost to a boil then immediately remove from heat.

PREPARATION TIME: 45 MINUTES   SERVES: 6 TO 8

Chicken Vindaloo

 Vindaloo (or vinthaleaux) originated in the Portuguese colony of Goa along the west coast of India. The Portuguese are credited with introducing vinegar, a key component in this dish, to Indian cooking. It's a hot and sour curry (pictured on page 112) enriched with a touch of coconut milk.

2 pounds (900g) boneless, skinless chicken thighs or about 3 pounds (1,350g) with bone and skin

Spice mixture

    6 teaspoons ground coriander

    2 teaspoons ground cumin

    ½ teaspoon ground red pepper (cayenne)

    ½ teaspoon ground black pepper

    ¼ teaspoon ground turmeric

    ⅛ teaspoon ground cinnamon

    ⅛ teaspoon ground cloves

¼ cup white vinegar

2 cups (360g) thinly sliced onion

¼ cup (60 ml) vegetable oil

2 teaspoons minced garlic

2 teaspoons minced ginger

1 medium boiling potato, peeled and cut into ¾-inch (2 cm) cubes (about 1 cup; 170g)

½ teaspoon mustard seeds, coarsely ground with a mortar and pestle

1 cup (225g) chopped tomatoes, fresh or canned, drained

¼ cup (60 ml) canned unsweetened coconut milk

2 or 3 green chilies (serrano, Thai, or jalapeño), split lengthwise

2 teaspoons salt

Trim boneless, skinless chicken thighs of fat and cut into 1½-inch (4 cm) chunks. If only thighs with bone and skin are available, remove skin and fat and cut thighs into 2 or 3 pieces each, bone in. Rub chicken pieces with mixture of ground spices and vinegar, and let stand for 30 minutes.

In a Dutch oven or flameproof casserole over medium-high heat, fry onion in oil until edges are nicely browned. Add garlic and ginger and stir for 2 minutes until the onion is medium brown.

Add potato, mustard seeds, tomatoes, coconut milk, green chilies, and salt and stir for another 2 minutes. Add marinated chicken and ½ cup (120 ml) water and bring to a boil. Turn down heat and simmer, partially covered, for 30 minutes, or until chicken and potatoes are done. Sauce will not be thick. Taste for salt.

PREPARATION TIME: 1 HOUR 15 MINUTES, PLUS 30 MINUTES MARINATING TIME   SERVES: 6 TO 8

Chicken Masala

This North Indian–inspired chicken curry has a lively, thick sauce. The chicken pieces are rubbed with spices and browned in oil before the other ingredients are added to the pot.

2 pounds (900g) boneless, skinless chicken thighs or about 3 pounds (1,350g) with bone and skin

Spice mixture

    6 teaspoons ground coriander

    2 teaspoons ground cumin

    ½ teaspoon ground red pepper (cayenne)

    ½ teaspoon ground black pepper

    ½ teaspoon ground turmeric

1 teaspoon salt

2 cups (340g) thinly sliced onion

3 tablespoons vegetable oil

2 teaspoons minced garlic

2 teaspoons minced ginger

2 tablespoons vegetable oil, or more as needed

2 cups (450g) chopped tomatoes, fresh or canned, drained

1 teaspoon salt

2 teaspoons poppy seeds, coarsely ground in a mortar and pestle

½ cup (120 ml) water

⅛ teaspoon Garam Masala (page 171)

Trim boneless, skinless thighs of fat and cut into 2-inch (5 cm) chunks. If only thighs with bone and skin are available, remove skin and fat and cut thighs into 2 or 3 pieces each, bone in. Rub chicken pieces with mixture of ground spices and 1 teaspoon salt and refrigerate for 1 hour.

In a deep heavy frying pan or Dutch oven over medium-high heat, fry onion in 3 tablespoons oil until edges are nicely browned. Add garlic and ginger and stir for 2 minutes until onion turns medium brown. Remove onion mixture from pan and set aside.

Add 2 tablespoons oil (more if needed) to pan and heat over medium heat. Add chicken pieces and stir for 5 minutes, or until lightly browned. Add fried onion, tomatoes, and 1 teaspoon salt and simmer until tomato pieces become very soft.

Stir in crushed poppy seeds and water and bring to a boil. Turn down heat, cover, and simmer for 20 minutes.

Uncover and continue simmering for another 20 minutes, until sauce thickens and turns a darker shade of brown. Stir in garam masala, simmer for 1 minute, and remove from heat. Taste for salt.

PREPARATION TIME: 1 HOUR,
PLUS 1 HOUR MARINATING TIME   SERVES: 6 TO 8

Tandoori Chicken

 A tandoor *is a deep clay oven from North India designed for cooking breads and marinated meats at a very high temperature. The intense heat of the* tandoor *seals in moisture, resulting in succulent pieces of meat that are dry on the outside. The bright red color associated with this dish (pictured on page 112) comes from coloring agents not present in this recipe. Instead we use paprika, which turns the chicken a pale shade of orange.*

4 chicken breast halves and 8 drumsticks

1 tablespoon finely grated garlic

1 teaspoon finely grated ginger

2 teaspoons paprika

½ teaspoon fennel seeds, finely ground with a mortar and pestle

Spice mixture

  4 teaspoons ground coriander

  1 teaspoon ground cumin

  ¾ teaspoon ground red pepper (cayenne)

  ⅛ teaspoon ground black pepper

  ⅛ teaspoon ground cinnamon

  ⅛ teaspoon ground cloves

2 teaspoons fresh lemon juice

2 teaspoons salt

¼ cup (60 ml) plain low-fat yogurt

¼ cup (60 ml) sour cream

2 tablespoons vegetable oil

3 tablespoons melted unsalted butter

1 medium red or white onion, cut into rings

1 lime, cut into thin wedges

Twenty-four hours before serving, skin chicken and cut each breast half in half. Make deep slits (diagonal on the drumstick) 1 inch (2½ cm) apart on each piece and halfway to the bone.

In a large bowl combine garlic, ginger, paprika, fennel seeds, spice mixture, lemon juice, salt, yogurt, sour cream, and oil. Add chicken pieces and toss, making sure marinade gets into each slit. Cover bowl and leave in the refrigerator up to 24 hours, turning pieces over at least once during this period.

Preheat oven to 500°F (260°C; mark 10) or prepare grill (see note).

An hour before serving, wipe excess marinade off chicken. Place on a broiling pan (grill) and bake in preheated oven for 25 to 30 minutes (see note). Halfway through baking, turn pieces, basting both sides with melted butter. Chicken should be tender and moist, but not pink inside.

Serve garnished with onion rings and lime wedges.

Note: Alternatively, chicken may be cooked on an open grill, 5 to 6 inches (13 to 15 cm) above the hot coals.

PREPARATION TIME: 35 MINUTES,
PLUS MARINATING TIME   SERVES: 6 TO 8

Chicken Tikka

 The marinade here is similar to the one for the preceding Tandoori Chicken, except that it contains no yogurt. And because the chicken pieces (boneless chunks of dark meat) are small, less time is needed for marinating. These tender pieces of chicken, threaded on skewers and then broiled or grilled, make nice hors d'oeuvres.

2 pounds (900g) boneless, skinless
   chicken thighs
½ cup (120 ml) vegetable oil
2 teaspoons finely grated garlic
1 teaspoon finely grated ginger
Spice mixture
    4 teaspoons ground coriander
    2 teaspoons ground cumin
    ¼ teaspoon ground red pepper (cayenne)
    ¼ teaspoon ground black pepper
    ⅛ teaspoon ground cinnamon
    ⅛ teaspoon ground cloves
    ⅛ teaspoon ground cardamom
2 teaspoons fresh lemon juice
1½ to 2 teaspoons salt

3 tablespoons melted unsalted butter

1 medium white onion, cut into rings
1 lime, cut into thin wedges

If using bamboo skewers, soak for 2 to 3 hours beforehand to prevent burning.

Trim boneless, skinless chicken thighs of fat and cut into 1½-inch (4 cm) chunks. Marinate chicken in mixture of oil, garlic, ginger, spice mixture, lemon juice, and salt for at least 1 hour.

Preheat oven broiler (grill) or prepare open grill (see note).

Thread chicken pieces onto bamboo (soaked and drained) or metal skewers. Place skewers on a broiling pan (grill) 3 inches (8 cm) from heat, and broil (grill) 5 minutes on the first side and 3 minutes on the second. After turning, baste with melted butter. Chicken should be tender and moist but not pink inside.

Serve on warm platter, garnished with onion rings and wedges of lime.

Note: Alternatively, skewers may be cooked on an open grill, 5 to 6 inches (13 to 15 cm) above the hot coals, turning and basting as directed above.

PREPARATION TIME: 30 MINUTES,
PLUS 1 HOUR MARINATING TIME   SERVES: 6 TO 8

Egg Masala

 Outside India eggs and curry may not be associated, but we frequently serve hard-boiled eggs this way. Lightly toasted coriander, fennel seeds, and a bit of coconut milk make this sauce very flavorful. Halved boiled eggs are added to the sauce at the end and heated just until warmed through.

8 extra-large eggs

2 tablespoons ground coriander

1 cup (180g) finely chopped onion
3 tablespoons vegetable oil
1 teaspoon minced garlic
1 teaspoon minced ginger

½ cup (115g) chopped tomatoes, fresh or
   canned, drained
Spice mixture
   ½ teaspoon ground cumin
   ½ teaspoon ground red pepper (cayenne)
   ½ teaspoon ground black pepper
   ¼ teaspoon ground turmeric
   1/16 teaspoon ground cinnamon
   1/16 teaspoon ground cloves
½ teaspoon fennel seeds, coarsely ground
   with a mortar and pestle
1 teaspoon salt
¼ cup (60 ml) water

½ cup (120 ml) canned unsweetened
   coconut milk
½ cup (120 ml) water

In a 4-quart (4 L) saucepan bring approximately 2 quarts (2 L) water to full boil; gently add eggs with slotted spoon. When water returns to a boil, set timer for 9 minutes.

While eggs are boiling, measure ground coriander into a small dry frying pan and turn heat to medium. Lightly toast coriander, stirring constantly, until it becomes aromatic, 2 to 3 minutes. Remove from heat and set aside.

After timer rings, remove eggs promptly and run under cold water. If eggs are overboiled, yolks start to turn gray. Shell eggs and cut lengthwise in half, preferably using a piece of thread, which makes a cleaner cut than a knife. Set aside.

In a large frying pan over medium-high heat, fry onion in oil until it turns light brown. Add garlic and ginger and stir 1 minute.

Add toasted coriander, tomatoes, spice mixture, fennel seeds, and salt and fry until tomato pieces become very soft and break up. Add ¼ cup (60 ml) water and simmer to produce a thick paste.

Bombay market

Stir in coconut milk and ½ cup (120 ml) water and continue to cook until the mixture becomes a moderately thick sauce. Taste for salt.

Place eggs, cut side up, in sauce. Spoon some of the sauce over eggs and bring to a boil. Turn heat down and simmer for 2 minutes.

Remove from heat and set aside, covered, for 15 minutes before serving.

PREPARATION TIME: 40 MINUTES   SERVES: 6 TO 8

Pitched gabled roof typical of Kerala architecture

Egg Aviyal

 This version of a classic Kerala dish aviyal *(pronounced ah-VEAL) is made with eggs and potatoes. It is best to grind the coconut to a fine consistency so it blends into the sauce.*

6 extra-large eggs

1 cup (115g) grated unsweetened coconut
¼ cup (45g) coarsely chopped onion
2 tablespoons plain low-fat yogurt
1 teaspoon salt
Spice mixture
    1 teaspoon ground coriander
    ¼ teaspoon ground cumin
    ½ teaspoon ground red pepper (cayenne)
    ¼ teaspoon ground turmeric
1 cup (240 ml) water, or more as needed

1 large boiling potato, peeled and cut
    lengthwise into finger-size pieces
    (about 1½ cups; 255g)

1 tablespoon vegetable oil
10 curry leaves or 4 bay leaves

In a 4-quart (4 L) saucepan bring approximately 2 quarts (2 L) water to a full boil; gently add eggs with a slotted spoon. When water returns to a boil, set timer for 9 minutes.

While eggs are boiling, combine coconut, onion, yogurt, salt, spice mixture, and 1 cup (240 ml) water in a food processor or blender, and grind to a fine consistency (a blender will require more water).

After timer rings, remove eggs promptly and run under cold water. If eggs are overboiled, yolks start to turn gray. Shell eggs and cut lengthwise in half with thread. Set aside.

In a deep frying pan combine coconut mixture and potato pieces; bring to boil, then turn heat down and simmer, partially covered, until potato is tender, about 12 minutes. Add more water as needed to prevent sticking.

Add oil and curry leaves; stir briefly. Taste for salt. Set eggs, cut side up, in sauce, between potatoes. Spoon some of sauce over eggs and bring to a boil. Turn heat down and let simmer for 1 minute.

Remove from heat and set aside, covered, for 15 minutes before serving.

PREPARATION TIME: 40 MINUTES   SERVES: 4 TO 6

Lamb, Beef, and Pork

ANCIENT ARCHEOLOGICAL EVIDENCE of sharp tools and animal bones found in the subcontinent indicate that the early inhabitants of India ate meat. But as the Hindu, Buddhist, and Jain religions evolved, the idea of taking a life for food was questioned. Food taboos, however, vary from one religion to the next. Buddhists and Jains shun meat altogether; most Hindus, Sikhs, and Parsis won't eat beef or pork but might eat fish, chicken, lamb, or goat; Muslims avoid pork but eat beef, lamb, goat, and chicken; Christians can eat all meat, including beef and pork. ▨ MEAT CURRIES in southwestern India are the pride of Kerala's and Goa's Christian communities. Nowhere else can one find flavorful meat dishes like *piralen,* a typical Syrian Christian dish in which chunks of lamb or beef are marinated in spices and vinegar, sautéed until the sauce is reduced to a glaze, and finished with fried onions, curry leaves, and mustard seeds. ▨ OTHER CULINARY TRADEMARKS of this region include fresh coconut, ginger, and hot chilies. Lamb Stew with Potatoes (page 129) illustrates how harmoniously these flavors blend with meat. A meat stew served with the rice pancakes called Appam (page 34) is typical breakfast fare in a Kerala Christian home. In Goa, where the Portuguese brought their brand of Christianity in the sixteenth century, pork dishes are the local specialty. One of the most famous Goan dishes is Pork Vindaloo (page 141), a hot and sour curry made with coconut, vinegar, and green chilies. This dish was a particular favorite

Clockwise from left: Spinach Lamb,
Pappadam, Pullao with Peas

of the British, who thought Goans were the best cooks in India.

Lamb Korma (page 135), Kofta (page 140), and Lamb Kabab (page 134) are classic North Indian meat preparations that owe their legacy to the Mughal chefs. *Korma* refers to a specific style of cooking—slowly braising meat in a creamy sauce to yield a thick curry. *Kofta* curry is seasoned ground meatballs simmered in a rich sauce. *Kababs* can be cubed marinated pieces of meat as in Lamb Kabab, or seasoned ground meat pressed into patties and served as a snack like Shami Kabab (page 45).

Spinach Lamb (page 137) also comes from the north, where lamb is eaten perhaps more often than anywhere else in India. The other meat used in curries is goat, called mutton in India. The well-known meat dish in a red sauce, Rogan Josh (page 138), is made with goat or lamb by Indian cooks, although this recipe uses lamb. A simple household curry is *keema,* which literally means "ground meat." The recipe in this chapter (page 139) is an easily prepared dish that my father makes with ground beef, potatoes, and peas.

Meat curries are best cooked in heavy pots and slowly simmered. A long cooking time ensures that the spices mellow and the meat becomes thoroughly tender. The sauces are formed with sautéed onions, garlic, and ginger; spices; and a minimum amount of cooking liquid, including the juices from the meat. Since the meat releases its juices gradually, don't be concerned if the amount of cooking liquid seems small at first; the finished dish will have plenty of sauce.

When using a leg of lamb, have the butcher remove the bone, but trim the meat yourself to make pieces the proper size. Allow about half an hour to trim and cut the meat in addition to the preparation time noted on the recipe. When using ground meat, the best, leanest choice is ground sirloin. Ground lamb has a nice flavor, but it is more difficult to find and not as lean as sirloin.

Lamb Stew with Potatoes

 A traditional Kerala stew, this flavorful blend of lamb and potatoes in a coconut milk sauce is seasoned with green chilies, curry leaves, and ginger. It is best eaten with porous pancakes like Appam (page 34) or Rava Dosa (page 32).

2 pounds (900 g) cubed leg of lamb trimmed of fat (about 4 cups 1-inch [2½ cm] cubes)
2 teaspoons all-purpose (plain) flour
2 tablespoons vegetable oil

1 cup (240 ml) water
½ cup (120 ml) canned unsweetened coconut milk
1 tablespoon white vinegar
1 teaspoon salt
3 green chilies (serrano, Thai, or jalapeño), split lengthwise
10 curry leaves or 4 bay leaves
1 tablespoon minced ginger

1 cup (180g) thinly sliced onion
2 tablespoons vegetable oil
2-inch (5 cm) piece cinnamon stick
4 whole cloves
⅛ teaspoon peppercorns, slightly crushed with a mortar and pestle

2 medium boiling potatoes, peeled and cut into ¾-inch (2 cm) cubes (about 2 cups; 340g)

½ cup (120 ml) canned unsweetened coconut milk

Toss lamb with flour to coat lightly. In a Dutch oven or flame-proof casserole over medium heat, fry lamb in 2 tablespoons oil, stirring constantly until all pink color disappears.

Add water, ½ cup (120 ml) coconut milk, vinegar, salt, green chilies, curry leaves, and ginger. Bring to a boil, turn heat down, and simmer, uncovered, for 15 minutes.

While meat mixture is simmering, in a frying pan over medium heat, fry onion in 2 tablespoons oil until soft. Add cinnamon, cloves, and crushed peppercorns. Fry 2 minutes, or until spices release their fragrance. Do not let onion brown.

Add onion mixture and cubed potatoes to meat and bring to a boil. Turn heat down and simmer, covered, for 20 minutes, or until potatoes are cooked. Sauce should be thick.

Stir in ½ cup (120 ml) coconut milk. Bring mixture almost to a boil, then immediately remove from heat.

PREPARATION TIME: 45 MINUTES   SERVES: 6 TO 8

Lamb Piralen

 This semidry curry of meat and potatoes glazed in a small amount of brown sauce is a Syrian Christian specialty and a Kerala favorite. Marinating meat in vinegar and spices is characteristic of Syrian Christian cooking. The vinegar adds a lively, sharp edge to the flavor. Serve with Okra Kichadi (page 85), Kootu (page 69), and Lemon Rice (page 147).

2 pounds (900g) cubed leg of lamb trimmed
   of fat (about 4 cups ¾-inch [2 cm] cubes)

Spice mixture
   6 teaspoons ground coriander, lightly
      toasted (see note)
   ½ teaspoon ground cumin
   ½ teaspoon ground red pepper (cayenne)
   ½ teaspoon ground black pepper
   ¼ teaspoon ground turmeric
   ⅛ teaspoon ground cinnamon
   ⅛ teaspoon ground cloves
½ teaspoon fennel seeds, coarsely ground
   with a mortar and pestle
1½ tablespoons white vinegar

Salt
2 medium boiling potatoes, peeled and cut
   into ¾-inch (2 cm) cubes (about 2 cups;
   340g)

½ cup (90g) thinly sliced onion
⅓ cup (80 ml) vegetable oil
2 teaspoons minced garlic
2 teaspoons minced ginger

Marinate lamb in mixture of ground spices, fennel seeds, and vinegar for at least 1 hour.

In a saucepan of salted water, parboil cubed potatoes for 12 minutes; set aside.

In a large heavy frying pan over medium-high heat, fry ½ cup (90g) sliced onion in ⅓ cup (80 ml) oil until edges are nicely browned. Add garlic and ginger and stir for 2 minutes, or until onion turns medium brown.

Add marinated lamb and stir until meat is no longer pink. Add 1¼ teaspoons salt and ¼ cup (60 ml) water, or enough to keep meat simmering. Cook, uncovered, over low heat for about 20 to 25 minutes, or until meat is tender and sauce is reduced to a very small amount.

Meanwhile, in a nonstick frying pan over medium-high heat, fry potatoes in 2 tablespoons oil until light brown, crusty, and cooked through, about 20 minutes. Add potatoes to lamb. Raise heat to medium-high and stir to coat thoroughly with sauce. Turn heat down to low.

1¼ teaspoons salt
¼ cup (60 ml) water, or more as needed

2 tablespoons vegetable oil

½ teaspoon mustard seeds
10 curry leaves or 2 bay leaves
2 tablespoons vegetable oil
¼ cup (45g) minced onion

In a small covered frying pan heat mustard seeds and curry leaves in 2 tablespoons oil over medium-high heat until mustard seeds begin to pop. Add ¼ cup (45g) onion and fry until it turns light brown. Pour contents of frying pan over lamb and potatoes, stir well, and remove from heat. Taste for salt.

Note: Toast ground coriander by stirring it in a dry frying pan over medium heat until it browns and becomes aromatic. Set aside to cool before using.

PREPARATION TIME: 1 HOUR 30 MINUTES,
PLUS 1 HOUR MARINATING TIME   SERVES: 6 TO 8

A floating Christian chapel on a Kerala canal

Lamb-Fry

 This simple lamb stir-fry (pictured opposite) is another Kerala specialty. It makes a nice light meal when paired with Puri (page 152) or Rava Dosa (page 32), or serve it with Dhal with Coconut (page 65), Spinach Pachadi (page 82), Sweet Potato Erisheri (page 72), and rice for a full meal.

2 cups (360g) thinly sliced onion

3 tablespoons vegetable oil

1 teaspoon minced garlic

1 teaspoon minced ginger

1 teaspoon minced green chili (serrano, Thai, or jalapeño)

Spice mixture

    3 teaspoons ground coriander

    ½ teaspoon ground cumin

    ¼ teaspoon ground red pepper (cayenne)

    ¼ teaspoon ground black pepper

    1/16 teaspoon ground turmeric

    1/16 teaspoon ground cinnamon

    1/16 teaspoon ground cloves

2 tablespoons water

2 pounds (900g) cubed leg of lamb trimmed of fat (about 4 cups ¾-inch [2 cm] cubes)

1 teaspoon salt

½ teaspoon fresh lemon juice

In a large nonstick frying pan over medium-high heat, fry onion in oil until edges are nicely browned. Add garlic, ginger, and green chili and stir for 1 minute.

Mix ground spices with water to form a paste; add to onion mixture. Stir briefly until spices release their fragrance.

Add lamb and salt and fry over medium heat, stirring frequently until lamb is cooked through, 10 to 15 minutes. Taste for salt.

Stir in lemon juice and remove from heat.

PREPARATION TIME: 30 MINUTES   SERVES: 4 TO 6

Lamb-Fry with Rava Dosa and Tomato and Cucumber Salad

Lamb Kabab

 An Indian variation on Middle Eastern shish kebab, these can be broiled in the oven or grilled over charcoal. For a more elaborate presentation, add cherry tomatoes, onions, and peppers to the marinade, and thread them on the skewers between the lamb pieces. For a simple dinner in the summertime, I serve this with Chutney for Kabab (page 61), pita bread, yogurt, and a green salad.

2 pounds (900g) cubed leg of lamb trimmed
    of fat (about 4 cups 1-inch [2½ cm] cubes)
⅓ cup (80 ml) vegetable oil
1 teaspoon finely grated garlic
2 teaspoons finely grated ginger
¼ teaspoon fennel seeds, finely ground with
    a mortar and pestle
Spice mixture
    4 teaspoons ground coriander
    1 teaspoon ground cumin
    ½ teaspoon ground red pepper (cayenne)
    ½ teaspoon ground black pepper
    ⅛ teaspoon ground cinnamon
    ⅛ teaspoon ground cloves
    ⅛ teaspoon cardamom
1¼ teaspoons salt
¼ cup (60 ml) tomato sauce

¼ cup (60 ml) melted unsalted butter

If using bamboo skewers, soak for 2 or 3 hours beforehand to prevent burning.

Marinate lamb cubes in mixture of oil, garlic, ginger, fennel seeds, ground spices, salt, and tomato sauce for at least 1 hour.

Thread meat cubes on bamboo (soaked and drained) or metal skewers. Broil or grill, 5 to 6 inches from heat, for about 7 minutes. Rotate skewers, baste with butter, and cook 5 more minutes, or until pieces are cooked through; continue basting if meat appears dry.

PREPARATION TIME: 30 MINUTES,
PLUS 1 HOUR MARINATING TIME   SERVES: 6 TO 8

Lamb Korma

 Korma *is a rich meat (or vegetable) curry cooked in a deliciously creamy sauce. This lamb version, one of the most celebrated of Mughal dishes, was introduced to the south by the Muslims who settled there.*

2 pounds (900g) cubed leg of lamb trimmed of fat (about 4 cups 1-inch [2½ cm] cubes)
Spice mixture
    6 teaspoons ground coriander
    1 teaspoon ground cumin
    ½ teaspoon ground red pepper (cayenne)
    ½ teaspoon ground black pepper
    ¼ teaspoon ground turmeric
½ cup (120 ml) sour cream

3 cups (540g) thinly sliced onion
4 tablespoons vegetable oil
2 tablespoons unsalted butter
2-inch (5 cm) piece cinnamon stick
4 whole cloves
4 cardamom pods, crushed lightly to break pods
2 teaspoons minced garlic
2 teaspoons minced ginger

¼ teaspoon fennel seeds, coarsely ground with a mortar and pestle
¼ cup (60 ml) canned unsweetened coconut milk
1½ teaspoons salt
¾ cup (180 ml) water, or more as needed

1 teaspoon fresh lemon juice

Marinate lamb in mixture of ground spices and sour cream for 30 minutes.

In a Dutch oven or flameproof casserole over medium-high heat, fry onion in mixture of oil and butter until edges are nicely browned. Add cinnamon, cloves, cardamom, garlic, and ginger and continue frying for 1 or 2 minutes until onion turns medium brown.

Add marinated lamb to onion mixture and stir over medium to medium-high heat until sour cream disappears and lamb is no longer pink on the outside, about 2 minutes. Stir in crushed fennel seeds, coconut milk, salt, and ¾ cup (180 ml) water; bring to a boil. Turn heat down and simmer, covered, for 30 minutes.

Uncover and simmer for another 20 to 25 minutes to thicken sauce, adding more water if sauce is too thick. At this point the meat and sauce should have darkened somewhat.

Stir in lemon juice and remove from heat. Taste for salt.

PREPARATION TIME: 1 HOUR 15 MINUTES, PLUS 30 MINUTES MARINATING TIME   SERVES: 6 TO 8

Spinach and other vegetables at an outdoor market

Spinach Lamb

The combination of tender lamb pieces and thick spinach sauce produces this superior North Indian meat curry (pictured on page 126). My father has been cooking this dish for years, and it never fails to win over those who taste it. Serve it with Eggplant and Tomatoes (page 95), Potatoes and Bell Peppers (page 90), Raita (page 57), Puri (page 152), and Basmati Rice (page 145).

2 pounds (900g) cubed leg of lamb trimmed
   of fat (about 4 cups 1-inch [2½ cm] cubes)
Spice mixture
   4 teaspoons ground coriander
   1 teaspoon ground cumin
   ½ teaspoon ground red pepper (cayenne)
   ½ teaspoon ground black pepper
   ¼ teaspoon ground turmeric
½ cup (120 ml) plain low-fat yogurt

1 package (10 ounces; 285g) frozen chopped
   spinach, thawed and partially drained
1 cup (240 ml) milk
1 teaspoon salt

2 cups (360g) coarsely chopped onion
¼ cup vegetable oil
2-inch (5 cm) piece cinnamon stick, broken
   in half
6 whole cloves
2 teaspoons minced garlic
2 teaspoons minced ginger

¼ teaspoon fennel seeds, coarsely ground
   with a mortar and pestle
1 cup (240 ml) water
1 teaspoon salt
1 teaspoon fresh lemon juice

Marinate lamb in mixture of ground spices and yogurt for 30 minutes.

In a 2-quart (2 L) saucepan over medium-high heat, cook spinach with milk and 1 teaspoon salt until almost all milk has boiled away, being careful not to burn. Set aside.

In a Dutch oven or flameproof casserole over medium-high heat, fry onion in oil until edges are nicely browned. Add cinnamon, cloves, garlic, and ginger and stir 1 to 2 minutes until onion turns medium brown.

Add marinated lamb to onion mixture and stir over medium to medium-high heat until yogurt disappears and lamb is no longer pink on the outside, about 2 minutes. Add cooked spinach, fennel seeds, water, and 1 teaspoon salt and bring to a boil. Turn heat down to low and simmer, covered, for 45 minutes.

Uncover and cook another 10 minutes over medium heat to thicken sauce. At this point, meat and sauce should have darkened somewhat.

Stir in lemon juice and remove from heat. Taste for salt.

PREPARATION TIME: 1 HOUR 30 MINUTES,
PLUS 30 MINUTES MARINATING TIME   SERVES: 6 TO 8

Rogan Josh

 This elegant Mughal meat dish traditionally derives its red color from Kashmiri red pepper or the cock's comb flower, according to some, but here paprika and tomato make it red. The robust sauce is thickened with ground poppy seeds.

2 pounds (900g) cubed leg of lamb trimmed of fat (about 4 cups 1-inch [2½ cm] cubes)
Spice mixture
    6 teaspoons ground coriander
    1 teaspoon ground cumin
    ½ teaspoon ground red pepper (cayenne)
    ½ teaspoon ground black pepper
    ¼ teaspoon ground turmeric
½ cup (120 ml) plain low-fat yogurt

2 cups (360g) thinly sliced onion
¼ cup (60 ml) vegetable oil
2 teaspoons minced garlic
2 teaspoons minced ginger
2 cups (450g) chopped tomatoes, fresh or canned, drained
2 teaspoons salt

1 tablespoon poppy seeds, ground with a mortar and pestle
Spice mixture
    1 teaspoon paprika
    ⅛ teaspoon ground cinnamon
    ⅛ teaspoon ground cloves
    ⅛ teaspoon grated or ground nutmeg
    ⅛ teaspoon ground mace
½ cup (120 ml) water

¼ teaspoon fresh lemon juice

Marinate lamb in mixture of ground spices—coriander, cumin, red pepper, black pepper, turmeric—and yogurt for at least 1 hour.

In a Dutch oven or flameproof casserole over medium-high heat, fry onion in oil until edges are nicely browned. Add garlic and ginger and stir for 2 minutes. Add tomato and salt and fry, stirring constantly, until tomato pieces become very soft and break up.

Add marinated lamb and stir over medium to medium-high heat until yogurt disappears and lamb is no longer pink, about 2 minutes. Stir in poppy seeds and other ground spices—paprika, cinnamon, cloves, nutmeg, and mace. Add water and bring to a boil. Turn heat down to low and simmer, covered, for 45 minutes.

Uncover and cook another 10 minutes over medium heat to thicken sauce. At this point, meat and sauce should appear somewhat darker.

Add the lemon juice, stir for another minute, and remove from heat.

PREPARATION TIME: 1 HOUR 30 MINUTES, PLUS 1 HOUR MARINATING TIME   SERVES: 6 TO 8

Keema

Keema, *a ground meat curry made with either beef or lamb, is an easy dish that cooks more quickly than other meat curries. It goes especially well with Puri (page 152) and a thick North Indian vegetable curry like Eggplant Bhurta (page 96) or Spinach Paneer (page 80).*

2 cups (360g) thinly sliced onion

¼ cup (60 ml) vegetable oil

2 teaspoons minced garlic

2 teaspoons minced ginger

1½ pounds (675g) very lean ground beef
    or lamb

Spice mixture

    6 teaspoons ground coriander

    1 teaspoon ground cumin

    ½ teaspoon ground red pepper (cayenne)

    ½ teaspoon ground black pepper

    ¼ teaspoon ground turmeric

    ⅛ teaspoon ground cinnamon

    ⅛ teaspoon ground cloves

1 to 2 chilies (serrano, Thai, or jalapeño),
    split lengthwise

2 teaspoons salt

2 medium boiling potatoes, peeled and cut
    into ¾-inch (2 cm) cubes (about 2 cups;
    340g)

1 cup (225g) chopped tomatoes, fresh or
    canned, drained

1 cup (240 ml) water

1 cup (135g) frozen peas

1 teaspoon fresh lemon juice

In a large frying pan over medium-high heat, fry onion in oil until edges are nicely browned. Add garlic and ginger and stir 2 minutes, or until onion turns medium brown. Add ground meat and fry until it browns, stirring to completely break up lumps.

Stir in spice mixture, green chilies, and salt until well blended. Add potatoes, tomatoes, and water; bring to boil. Turn heat down to low and simmer, partially covered, for 30 minutes.

Add peas and cook, uncovered, for another 5 minutes. Mixture should be neither dry nor watery. If it seems dry, add a little water; if it seems watery, continue cooking with lid off.

Stir in lemon juice and remove from heat. Taste for salt.

PREPARATION TIME: 1 HOUR   SERVES: 6 TO 8

Kofta

 In this North Indian meat curry, ground beef or lamb is formed into balls that are braised in a fragrant sauce. Preparing the meatballs is an extra step, but worth the effort.

1 pound (450g) very lean ground beef (or lamb)
1 teaspoon grated ginger
1 tablespoon grated onion
½ teaspoon ground coriander
½ teaspoon salt
1 large egg, lightly beaten
½ cup (60g) plain dry bread crumbs
Vegetable oil for frying

1 cup (180g) finely chopped onion
3 tablespoons vegetable oil
1 teaspoon minced garlic
½ teaspoon minced ginger
1 teaspoon minced green chili (serrano,
    Thai, or jalapeño)

1 cup chopped tomatoes, fresh or canned,
    drained

Spice mixture
    1 teaspoon ground coriander
    ½ teaspoon ground cumin
    ½ teaspoon ground red pepper (cayenne)
    ½ teaspoon ground black pepper
    ⅛ teaspoon ground turmeric
    ⅛ teaspoon grated or ground nutmeg
    ⅛ teaspoon ground mace
¾ teaspoon salt
¾ cup (180 ml) water, or more as needed

¼ teaspoon Garam Masala (page 171)

In a large bowl combine meat, 1 teaspoon ginger, 1 tablespoon onion, ½ teaspoon ground coriander, ½ teaspoon salt, egg, and bread crumbs. Mix well. Make into 1-inch (2½ cm) balls (about 16). Brown in a very small amount of oil in a nonstick frying pan over medium-high heat, shaking pan frequently so meatballs brown on all sides. When they are nicely browned, remove from the pan to paper towels to drain.

In a Dutch oven or flameproof casserole, over medium-high heat, fry onion in oil until edges are nicely browned. Add garlic, ginger, and green chili and stir for 2 minutes until onion turns medium brown.

Add tomatoes, spice mixture, and salt and stir constantly until tomato pieces become very soft and break up. Add ¾ cup (180 ml) water and bring to a boil. Add the meatballs, turn heat down to low, and simmer for 45 minutes, adding more water as necessary to keep sauce from drying out. Sauce should be moderately thick at the end.

Add garam masala and simmer for another minute before removing from heat. Taste for salt.

PREPARATION TIME: 1 HOUR 30 MINUTES   SERVES: 6

Pork Vindaloo

 This famous dish originates from Goa, north of Karnataka on the Malabar Coast. Goa was a Portuguese colony in the fifteenth and sixteenth centuries, during which time the local Hindus either converted to Christianity or fled. Unlike Hindus and Muslims, Christians have no religious taboos against eating pork, so this is one of a handful of pork specialties from India. Its characteristic hot and sour flavors come from green chilies and vinegar. This version is fairly hot, but the amount of chili can be adjusted to taste.

2 pounds (900g) pork tenderloin, cut into
1-inch (2½ cm) cubes

Spice mixture
   6 teaspoons ground coriander
   1 teaspoon ground cumin
   ½ teaspoon ground red pepper (cayenne)
   ½ teaspoon ground black pepper
   ¼ teaspoon ground turmeric
   ⅛ teaspoon ground cinnamon
   ⅛ teaspoon ground cloves
¼ cup (60 ml) white vinegar

2 cups (360g) thinly sliced onion
¼ cup (60 ml) vegetable oil
2 teaspoons minced garlic
2 teaspoons minced ginger

1 cup (225g) chopped tomatoes, fresh or
   canned, drained
½ teaspoon mustard seeds, coarsely ground
   with a mortar and pestle
¼ cup (60 ml) canned unsweetened
   coconut milk
2 to 3 green chilies (serrano, Thai, or
   jalapeño), split lengthwise
2 teaspoons salt
½ cup (120 ml) water, or more as needed

Marinate pork in mixture of ground spices and vinegar for at least 1 hour.

In a Dutch oven or flameproof casserole over medium-high heat, fry onion in oil until edges are nicely browned. Add garlic and ginger and stir for 2 minutes until onion is medium brown.

Add marinated pork, tomatoes, mustard seeds, coconut milk, green chilies, and salt and stir for 2 minutes. Add ½ cup (120 ml) water and bring to a boil. Turn heat down and simmer, covered, for 30 minutes or until the meat is cooked through but not dry. Stir occasionally; add a little water if mixture begins to dry out. Sauce should be moderately thick.

Remove from heat. Taste for salt.

PREPARATION TIME: 1 HOUR,
PLUS 1 HOUR MARINATING TIME   SERVES: 6 TO 8

Rice and Breads

In Kerala, where networks of canals crisscross the land, rice grows plentifully and is eaten as often as three times a day. A short, red-flecked variety is boiled and served with *dhal* (cooked legumes), curries, and *pappadam* (crisp flat lentil wafers) as the main meal of the day. Ground rice is also part of the fermented batter for *idli, dosa,* and *appam,* eaten for breakfast and light meals. From breakfast to dessert, Indian cooks have found innumerable uses for this adaptable grain.

The state of Tamil Nadu boasts exquisite flavored rice dishes like Coconut Rice (page 146), Lemon Rice (page 147), and Yogurt Rice (page 148), prepared for festive occasions. For a very special feast all three of these might be served together. Along with mustard seeds and curry leaves, these rich dishes feature fried *urad dhal* as a seasoning, contributing flavor as well as texture. Any standard long-grain white rice (not basmati, which is too flavorful) works well for these recipes. Aromatic basmati, the rice of choice in North India, is grown in the shadow of the Himalayas in the state of Uttar Pradesh. Its delicate flavor, often described as nutty, improves with at least six months of aging, and it is prized for the light, dry texture of the steamed grains. While tasty on its own, basmati is outstanding in such dishes as *pullao* and *biriyani.* In *pullao* rice is steamed with spices and vegetables. Biriyani (page 150) is a more elaborate preparation of savory rice, spiced meat, and fried onions, layered in a large pot and steamed together until the flavors are blended, and finally garnished with sautéed nuts and raisins.

Clockwise from top: Saffron Rice, Lemon Rice, Yogurt Rice, Pullao with Peas, Coconut Rice

All Indian-grown rice should be rinsed well in cold water prior to cooking. This process removes unwanted particles and also washes away excess starch, allowing the grains to separate as they cook.

Next to rice, wheat is India's second largest crop. Unleavened wheat breads like Puri (fried, puffed bread; page 152) and Chappathi (flat griddle-cooked bread; page 154) are staples of the North Indian diet, rather than rice. Punjab, often called "the breadbasket of India," is the primary wheat-growing state in the country, and from Punjabi mills comes the country's finest *atta* flour. *Atta* (sold at Indian grocery stores) is processed from low-gluten durum wheat, and is preferred for making *puri* and *chappathi*. In the north breads are eaten as the sole starch of the meal or with rice at a more elaborate dinner.

Long-Grain Rice

Rice is an important element in an Indian meal, especially in the south, where it's eaten in a number of different forms, three meals a day. South Indians put a huge scoop of plain boiled rice on their plate, top it with ghee, *and surround it with* dhal *and bits of curries. The rice acts as a neutral base against which the highly seasoned dishes are enjoyed. To cleanse the palate, a final serving of rice is eaten mixed with yogurt. The appetite for rice in the south is so immense that one of the first Malayalam words I learned in Kerala was "Mathi!" ("Enough!"), because if I didn't stop her, my aunt would serve me piles of rice with every course.*

4 cups (960 ml) water
1½ teaspoons salt
2 cups (340g) long-grain rice

In a 3-quart (3 L) saucepan over high heat, bring water to a boil. Add salt and rice and continue to heat until water begins to boil again. Stir to break up lumps.

Turn heat down to low and cover tightly. (If lid appears loose, weigh it down with any handy weight.) Simmer for 35 minutes, without removing lid, until water is absorbed and rice is cooked through. Rice should be fluffy, not sticky or dry.

PREPARATION TIME: 45 MINUTES   SERVES: 6 TO 8

Basmati Rice

This celebrated rice from North India has a nutty flavor and delicate texture. Imported basmati rice purchased from an Indian grocery store must be rinsed several times and checked for grit and particles. Its transplanted American versions, Texmati and Kasmati rice, are widely available in grocery stores and require no such cleaning.

I've encountered many methods for cooking basmati—all designed to maximize its fluffiness. While there are more complicated ways that may produce airier results, this simple method works well. Washing the rice first helps to separate the grains because it removes the starch that causes them to stick together. Basmati is excellent plain or in pullao, *but because of its aromatic flavor is not recommended for the South Indian rice dishes in this book flavored with lemon, coconut, and yogurt.*

2 cups (340g) basmati rice
3½ cups (830 ml) water
1½ teaspoons salt

Wholesale rice distributor in Cochin

Rinse basmati by placing it in a large bowl, and then fill bowl with water and drain it off repeatedly until water is no longer cloudy. Drain rice completely.

In a 3-quart (3 L) saucepan over high heat, bring rice, 3½ cups (840 ml) water, and salt to a boil with cover off. Stir briefly, then cover tightly (weighing down lid, if necessary), turn heat down to low, and simmer for 20 minutes. Do not remove lid while cooking.

Remove from heat and let stand 10 minutes with cover on tight.

PREPARATION TIME: 40 MINUTES   SERVES: 6

Coconut Rice

 Our friend Yoga has a deft hand with flavored rice dishes. She gave us this recipe (pictured on pages 98 and 142), along with those for the following Lemon Rice and Yogurt Rice. Toasted coconut gives this one a rich aroma. It goes particularly well with fish and shrimp curries.

½ cup (60g) split urad dhal

4 cups (960 ml) water
1½ teaspoons salt
2 cups (340g) long-grain rice

1 teaspoon mustard seeds
4 dried red peppers
10 curry leaves or 4 bay leaves
½ cup (120 ml) vegetable oil
½ cup (60g) broken raw cashew nuts
1 cup (115g) grated unsweetened coconut
¼ teaspoon asafetida (optional)
½ teaspoon salt

2 tablespoons Ghee (page 172)

Rinse urad dhal and soak in a bowl of water for 1 hour. Drain and set aside.

In a large saucepan prepare rice according to recipe on page 144.

While rice is cooking, heat mustard seeds, red peppers, and curry leaves in oil over medium-high heat in a covered wok or large frying pan until mustard seeds begin to pop. Uncover and immediately add soaked urad dhal, cashew nuts, coconut, asafetida, and salt. Fry for about 10 minutes, or until nuts and urad dhal turn a light reddish brown and coconut becomes golden.

Remove from heat and stir in ghee. Add cooked rice and stir in gently but thoroughly.

Serve hot or at room temperature.

PREPARATION TIME: 50 MINUTES,
PLUS 1 HOUR SOAKING TIME FOR URAD DHAL   SERVES: 8

Kerala rice fields

Lemon Rice

 This spicy rice dish (pictured on page 142) resonates with lemon. Turmeric turns it a pretty shade of yellow, and sautéed yellow split peas and urad dhal *give it a crunchy quality. This one enhances any meal, Indian or otherwise.*

4 cups (960 ml) water
1½ teaspoons salt
2 cups (340g) long-grain rice

1 teaspoon mustard seeds
4 dried red peppers
10 curry leaves or 4 bay leaves
½ cup (120 ml) vegetable oil

2 tablespoons yellow split peas
2 tablespoons split urad dhal
½ cup broken raw cashew nuts
1 cup (180g) chopped onion
1 cup (115g) coarsely chopped green bell
   pepper
1 teaspoon minced green chili (serrano,
   Thai, or jalapeño), or less to taste
2 teaspoons minced ginger
¼ teaspoon ground turmeric
⅛ teaspoon asafetida (optional)
1 teaspoon salt

¼ cup (60 ml) fresh lemon juice

In a 3-quart (3 L) saucepan prepare rice according to recipe on page 144.

While rice is cooking, heat mustard seeds, red peppers, and curry leaves in oil over medium-high heat in a covered wok or large frying pan until mustard seeds begin to pop.

Uncover and immediately add split peas, urad dhal, cashews, onion, bell pepper, chili, ginger, turmeric, asafetida, and salt. Fry for 10 minutes, or until dhal and nuts turn reddish brown and bell pepper is tender.

Remove from heat and stir in lemon juice. Add cooked rice and stir in gently but thoroughly.

Serve hot or at room temperature.

PREPARATION TIME: 1 HOUR   SERVES: 8

Yogurt Rice

Serve this moist rice dish at room temperature for the best texture and flavor. We add a little sour cream for an extra-creamy consistency, but you can use all yogurt if you prefer. It goes well with some of the drier curries like Kerala Fried Fish (page 103), Lamb Piralen (page 130), or Chicken Tikka (page 121).

4 cups (960 ml) water
1½ teaspoons salt
2 cups (340g) long-grain rice

1 teaspoon mustard seeds
4 dried red peppers
10 curry leaves or 4 bay leaves
½ cup (120 ml) vegetable oil

2 tablespoons yellow split peas
2 tablespoons split urad dhal
½ cup (60g) broken raw cashew nuts
1 cup (180g) chopped onion
1 cup (115g) chopped red bell pepper
1 teaspoon minced green chili (serrano,
    Thai, or jalapeño), or less to taste
2 teaspoons minced ginger
1 teaspoon salt

2 cups (480 ml) plain low-fat yogurt
½ cup (120 ml) sour cream

In a 2-quart (2 L) saucepan prepare rice according to recipe on page 144.

In large covered wok or frying pan over medium-high heat, fry mustard seeds, red peppers, and curry leaves in oil until mustard seeds begin to pop.

Uncover and immediately add split peas, urad dhal, cashews, onion, bell pepper, chili, ginger, and salt. Fry for 10 minutes, or until dhal and nuts turn reddish brown and bell pepper is tender.

Remove from heat and stir in yogurt and sour cream. Add cooked rice and stir in gently but thoroughly.

Serve at room temperature.

PREPARATION TIME: I HOUR   SERVES: 8

Pullao with Peas

 Pullaos, *or seasoned rice dishes, came to India by way of ancient Muslim invaders, who knew them as pilafs. Mughal courtly cooks made them with spices and small pieces of meat and vegetable. Our simplified vegetarian version (pictured on page 142) is pleasantly scented with cinnamon, cloves, and cardamom. Without requiring much extra time to prepare, it's a nice change from plain rice. Serve with any of the curries in this book.*

1 medium onion, sliced

2 tablespoons vegetable oil

1-inch (2½ cm) piece cinnamon stick

4 whole cloves

4 cardamom pods, lightly crushed to
  break pods

⅛ teaspoon ground turmeric

4 cups (960 ml) water

2 cups (340g) long-grain rice (see note)

1½ teaspoons salt

1 cup (135g) frozen peas, thawed

In a large heavy pan over medium-high heat, fry onion in oil until it becomes light brown. Add cinnamon, cloves, cardamom, and turmeric and stir 1 minute.

Add water, turn heat to high, and bring to a boil. Add rice and salt and wait for water to boil again. Stir briefly to break up clumps. Turn heat down to low, cover tightly (weighing down lid if necessary), and simmer for 35 to 40 minutes, until water is absorbed and rice is cooked through.

Stir in peas, cover, and let sit on low heat for another 5 minutes.

Note: This may also be prepared with basmati rice. Rinse 2 cups (340g) basmati by placing it in a large bowl, then fill bowl with water and drain it off repeatedly until water is no longer cloudy. Drain rice completely. After frying spices as directed above, add 3½ cups (840 ml) water, rice, and 1½ teaspoons salt and bring to a boil. When mixture reaches a full boil, cover with a tight-fitting lid and reduce heat to very low; cook for 20 minutes. After 20 minutes, without removing lid, turn off heat and let rice sit for 5 minutes. Stir in peas, then re-cover and allow to sit another 5 minutes before serving.

PREPARATION TIME: 50 MINUTES   SERVES: 6 TO 8

Biriyani

Originally Persian, this elegant preparation of rice baked with spiced meat has become a mainstay of Kerala Muslim cuisine. My family's simplified version combines two recipes in this book, Saffron Rice and Chicken-Fry (or Lamb-Fry). This dish makes a stunning presentation.

Saffron Rice (page 151)

Chicken-Fry (page 115) or Lamb-Fry
  (page 132)

2 tablespoons low-fat yogurt

6 tablespoons unsalted butter

2 large onions, sliced

1 tablespoon Ghee (page 172)

4 hard-boiled eggs, quartered lengthwise

Prepare rice up to the point of preparing the nuts and raisins; golden raisins (sultanas) are prettiest for this dish. While rice is cooking, prepare the chicken or lamb, omitting lemon juice and adding yogurt to meat for final 2 minutes of cooking. Yogurt should blend in completely, producing a few tablespoons of sauce.

In a large frying pan over medium heat, melt butter. Add onion and fry until edges are golden brown. Set aside.

Preheat oven to 350°F (180°C; mark 4).

Brush bottom of Dutch oven or casserole with 1 tablespoon ghee, then add these ingredients, in layers, in following order:

- All meat pieces without their sauce
- Half of cooked Saffron Rice
- Sauce from meat spooned evenly over rice
- Remaining rice
- Fried onions spread in an even layer, plus 2 tablespoons of butter left over from cooking onions sprinkled over top

Tightly seal top of Dutch oven or casserole with aluminum foil, then place lid over foil. Bake in preheated oven for 30 minutes.

Meanwhile, fry nuts and raisins as for Saffron Rice.

Women working in a rice paddy

When rice and meat have baked for 30 minutes, carefully transfer to large serving platter, trying not to stir mixture too much. Garnish with sautéed nuts and raisins and wedges of hard-boiled egg.

PREPARATION TIME: 1 HOUR 45 MINUTES   SERVES: 8

Saffron Rice

 This golden rice dish (pictured on page 142) contains sautéed nuts and raisins. Though it is an expensive seasoning, there is no substitute for saffron's color and flavor. I prefer using basmati rice for this aromatic dish.

2 cups (340g) basmati rice

½ teaspoon saffron threads
2 tablespoons warm milk

1-inch (2½ cm) piece cinnamon stick
4 whole cloves
4 cardamom pods, crushed lightly to
    break pods
1 tablespoon vegetable oil
3¼ cups (780 ml) water
1½ teaspoons salt

⅓ cup (45g) broken raw cashew nuts or
    blanched slivered almonds
⅓ cup (45g) dark raisins or golden raisins
    (sultanas)
1 tablespoon Ghee (page 172) or butter

Rinse basmati by placing it in a large bowl, then fill bowl with water and drain it off repeatedly until water is no longer cloudy. Drain rice completely and set aside.

In a small bowl soak saffron in warm milk for 10 minutes.

In a 5- to 6-quart (5 to 6 L) saucepan over medium-high heat, fry cinnamon, cloves, and cardamom pods in oil for 1 to 2 minutes until they release their fragrance. Add rice, soaked saffron (with milk), water, and salt and bring to a full boil. Stir briefly to break up clumps.

Turn heat down to low, cover tightly (weighing down lid if necessary), and simmer, without removing lid, for 20 minutes. Turn off heat and allow rice to sit with cover on for 10 minutes. Fluff up rice with a fork.

In a small frying pan over medium heat, fry cashews or almonds and raisins in ghee or butter until nuts turn reddish brown. Stir thoroughly into rice and serve.

PREPARATION TIME: 45 MINUTES   SERVES: 6 TO 8

Puri

 Puri *are soft wheat breads that fill with air when fried. There are a few tricks to making a perfectly puffed* puri, *like rolling it to just the right thickness and having the oil precisely the right temperature, but only through practice will you get a feel for these variables. Using Indian* atta *flour made from durum wheat yields the best flavor and texture.*

Serve puri *with rice and curries for a large meal or serve alone with a potato or meat curry for a light snack. They should be fried just prior to serving, but they can be kept briefly wrapped in foil, if necessary.*

2 cups Indian atta flour or mixture of
    1⅓ cups (190g) all-purpose (plain) flour
    and ⅔ cup (100g) whole-wheat
    (wholemeal) flour
1 teaspoon salt
2 teaspoons vegetable oil
¾ to 1 cup (180 to 240 ml) warm water,
    or as needed

Vegetable oil for deep frying

In a medium bowl combine flour, salt, oil, and water to make stiff but pliable dough just soft enough to work into a smooth ball. (Exact amount of water needed may vary somewhat, but dough should be stiffer than bread dough.) Place in a clean bowl, cover with a wet cloth or paper towel, and let stand for 30 minutes.

Knead dough a few more times, then divide into 16 balls. Using a minimal amount of additional flour (all-purpose [plain]), dust your hands and work surface. Keeping remaining balls of dough covered, flatten one ball with the heel of your hand and roll it out with a lightly floured rolling pin to 5- to 6-inch (13 to 15 cm) diameter and about as thick as a tortilla. Use additional flour sparingly, otherwise dough becomes tough. Repeat procedure with remaining balls.

Heat oil in a wok or deep frying pan to 375°F (190°C; mark 5), or hot enough to cause a tiny ball of dough dropped in oil to rise quickly to the surface, releasing bubbles (see note). If oil starts to smoke, reduce heat.

A canal near Kottayam

Cooking one at a time, slip a rolled-out disc into hot oil and press it down gently with a slotted spoon to keep it submerged. Within ten seconds the puri should puff up like a balloon, or at least form large bubbles. (If it doesn't, the heat is too low.) Turn it over to cook the other side for a few more seconds, but do not submerge. Remove with slotted spoon to paper towels to drain.

Continue cooking puris, one at a time. They should be soft, easy to tear, and dry in appearance. Serve immediately, if possible, or keep warm and covered until ready to serve.

Note: Too much heat will cause the puris to become crisp and brown; too little will make them look oily and unpuffed.

PREPARATION TIME: 1 HOUR   SERVES: 6 TO 8
YIELD: SIXTEEN 6-INCH (15 CM) PURIS

Rice and Breads ※ 153

Chappathi

A staple of the north, this unadorned flat bread (pictured on page 112) is dry-roasted on a tava *(slightly concave iron griddle), but a nonstick or iron frying pan can also be used. Making them is a bit of a production because they cook in two stages, first on top of the griddle, then briefly over a heat source to puff them like balloons. The puffing step is not essential, but it produces a softer texture.*

2 cups Indian atta flour or mixture of
   1⅓ cups (190g) all-purpose (plain) flour
   and ⅔ cup (100g) whole-wheat
   (wholemeal) flour
1 teaspoon salt
¾ to 1 cup (180 to 240 ml) warm water
   (approximately)

Ghee (page 172)

In a medium bowl combine flour and salt and enough water to make a stiff but pliable dough that is just soft enough to work into a smooth ball. Dough should be soft but not sticky. (The exact amount of water needed may vary somewhat, but dough should be stiffer than bread dough.) Knead dough for 3 to 5 minutes until soft and pliable. Place in a clean bowl, covered with a wet cloth or paper towel, and let stand for 30 minutes.

Knead dough a few more times, then divide it into 16 balls roughly the size of Ping-Pong balls. Using a minimum amount of additional (all-purpose [plain]) flour, dust your hands and work surface. Keeping remaining balls covered, flatten one ball with heel of your hand and roll it out with a lightly floured rolling pin to a 5- to 6-inch (13 to 15 cm) diameter, and about as thick as a tortilla. Use additional all-purpose flour sparingly or dough will become tough. Place rolled discs on a cutting board slightly overlapping each other, and cover with a cloth.

For this step it's best to work rapidly and continually until all chappathis are cooked. If you stop at all, frying pan will

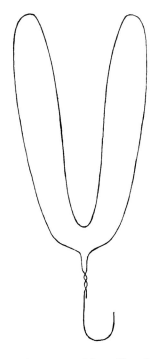

A wire hanger bent as a tool for puffing chappathis

overheat and burn flour particles on it. The process requires two burners, one for frying chappathis, the other for puffing them. For frying use a heavy frying pan or Indian *tava* on medium heat (hot enough to lightly brown grains of flour sprinkled on it). For puffing use a wire clothes hanger bent as follows (see diagram): Hold hanger with hook facing you. Keeping hanger in one plane, bend the long side in half and squeeze the two arms together to form "rabbit ears" or a narrow V, with bottom of V toward you. Have a basket with a cloth nearby, and a small pot of ghee with a spoon.

Place one disc of rolled dough in heated pan. Small bubbles of air will form in dough. Cook each side until a few brown spots appear on surface (about 20 to 30 seconds per side). Immediately place chappathi onto wire hanger so it is suspended horizontally. Using the hook as a handle, hold the chappathi 1 to 2 inches (2½ to 5 cm) over a second burner on high heat. (With a gas burner the flames may touch the chappathi but will not burn it in the short time needed for puffing.) Use caution, because hanger gets quite hot. In a few seconds chappathi should completely fill with air, like a balloon. Carefully turn chappathi over on hanger and briefly heat the other side. Slide chappathi into basket, spread top lightly with ghee, and keep covered with cloth. (Chappathi will deflate.) Repeat process, continuing to stack chappathis and spread their tops with ghee.

Serve immediately.

PREPARATION TIME: 1 HOUR   SERVES: 6 TO 8
YIELD: SIXTEEN 6-INCH (15 CM) CHAPPATHIS

Desserts and Beverages

WITH AFTERNOON TEA and on special occasions, Indians enjoy "sweetmeats" in a wide array of flavors and colors. One of the most beloved is a fudgelike candy called *burfi,* usually made from ground nuts or coconut cooked with *ghee* and milk. A delicious version, Almond Burfi (page 161), looks and tastes like marzipan. Another teatime sweet is *halva,* traditionally made from a grain or vegetable boiled in milk, then cooked with sugar and *ghee. Halva* tends to have a softer consistency than the crumbly *burfi.* Sooji Halva (page 164), made of *ghee,* farina, cashews, and raisins, has a slightly chewy texture, but others, like carrot *halva,* are soft enough to eat with a spoon. ▣ A FAVORITE South Indian sweetmeat, Mysore Pak (page 162) resembles shortbread and is made with roasted chickpea flour, which lends a lovely amber color and toasty flavor. While Mysore Pak would normally be served with tea, the dishing out of a dessert called *payasam* is reserved for truly special occasions. No birthday celebration in the south would be complete without a version of this milky pudding (see page 159 or 160). ▣ THE BENGALIS are renowned for creating some of India's finest confections, their skills passing from one generation to the next. *Ras malai,* milk-curd patties soaked in cream, were developed in the early twentieth century by the son of the Bengali sweetmaker who invented the porous milk cakes in syrup called *rasgolla.* Both of these are traditionally made from split milk curd, which is kneaded and pressed into small patties or balls. Another famous milk-based

Clockwise from center: Mango Lassi, South Indian Coffee, Gulab Jamun (top), Almond Burfi (bottom), Fried Bananas

Bengali sweet is *gulab jamun,* fried cakelike balls in sugar syrup. Although these desserts are reputed to be difficult to make, the adapted versions for Ras Malai (page 165) and Gulab Jamun (page 166) here are quite straightforward.

Tea, or *chai* as it is known in Hindi, has been brewed in India for centuries, but the ritual of "tea-time" was popularized by the British. The British had long enjoyed drinking Chinese tea, but found it did not grow well in Indian soil. Naturally, they were pleased to discover indigenous Indian tea plants flourishing in the northern states of Darjeeling and Assam; by the 1940s these regions were thick with plantations. In the north tea is often brewed with milk, water, spices, and sugar, and called Spiced Tea (page 168).

South Indian Coffee (page 169) is a bit like café au lait—a small amount of strongly brewed coffee diluted with hot, frothy milk. Coffee, which came to India by way of Arab traders, is primarily grown in the hilly regions of the south. Rich milky coffee is favored over tea by many in the south, especially with breakfast.

Cool yogurt drinks called *lassi* are rejuvenating on a hot day; these are enjoyed in the north during the dry summer months. Salty or sweet, they are shaken vigorously (or mixed in a blender) to give them the desired foamy consistency. They make a nourishing, if filling, refreshment. A version of sweet *lassi* made with mango (page 169) has garnered the most followers, especially since mangoes are believed to lower one's body temperature as well as quench one's thirst.

Milk Payasam

Payasam *(pronounced PAYA-sum) is a South Indian milk-based dessert (* kheer *in North India) with the consistency of thin pudding—usually served to celebrate special occasions like birthdays. This one made with rice gets very thick upon sitting; if you wish to thin it out, do so with a little warmed milk.*

2 quarts (1,900 ml) whole milk
¾ cup (130g) long-grain rice
½ teaspoon ground cardamom
⅛ teaspoon saffron (optional)

1¼ cups (240g) sugar
½ cup (60g) golden raisins (sultanas) or
   dark raisins
½ cup (60g) broken raw cashew nuts

In a heavy 5- to 6-quart (5 to 6 L) pot, boil milk, rice, cardamom, and saffron until rice is cooked and becomes soft. Over medium-high heat, this takes about 30 minutes. Stir frequently, especially during final 10 minutes.

Add sugar, raisins, and cashews and turn heat down to medium-low. Cook, stirring constantly, until mixture thickens, about 10 minutes. Remove from heat and set aside 3 to 6 hours before serving to allow payasam to thicken.

Serve warm.

PREPARATION TIME: 45 MINUTES,
NOT INCLUDING RESTING TIME   SERVES: 8 TO 10

Elephants decked out for a
Pongol *(harvest) celebration*

Vermicelli Payasam

 This type of payasam *uses fine noodles sautéed in ghee. Indian vermicelli is thinner than ours, so use angel hair (capellini) pasta. The flavor of this dessert improves with time, so make it a day ahead and thin it with a little warm milk before serving, since it thickens as it sits.*

1 teaspoon Ghee (page 172) or unsalted butter

1 cup (80g) angel hair pasta, broken into
 ¾-inch (2 cm) pieces

4 cups (960 ml) whole milk

2 cups (475 ml) water

¾ cup (105g) sugar

½ cup (60g) golden raisins (sultanas) or
 dark raisins

½ cup (60g) broken raw cashew nuts

2 teaspoons ghee or unsalted butter

¼ teaspoon ground cardamom

In a large frying pan heat 1 teaspoon ghee and pasta over medium heat until all pieces have lightly browned and give off a toasted aroma. Set aside.

In a 3-quart (3 L) heavy saucepan, heat milk and water on medium-high. As soon as mixture boils, reduce heat to medium and add fried pasta. Continue to simmer 6 minutes, or until pasta is well cooked. Add sugar and simmer 15 minutes, stirring frequently to prevent sticking. When mixture is done, it will have a creamy consistency.

While milk simmers, in frying pan used for pasta, fry raisins and cashews in 2 teaspoons ghee until lightly browned.

Add fried raisins and nuts and the cardamom to milk, stir, and remove from heat. Cover and set aside for a few hours or more.

Serve warm, reheating if necessary.

PREPARATION TIME: 35 MINUTES,
NOT INCLUDING RESTING TIME   SERVES: 8

Almond Burfi

 A wonderful candylike sweet (pictured on page 156) that tastes like marzipan with the added richness of ghee. It has a firm texture like fudge and will keep for 2 or 3 days in an airtight container.

1 cup (190g) sugar
½ cup (120 ml) water

1 pound (450g) almond paste, broken up to facilitate melting
Ghee (page 172), prepared from 8 ounces (2 sticks; 225g) unsalted butter

¼ cup (30g) sliced or slivered almonds chopped finer

In heavy 4-quart (4 L) pot combine sugar and water and boil together until candy thermometer registers 225°F (107°C) and small amount of the syrup forms a thin thread between the thumb and forefinger when carefully sampled from the stirrer.

Reduce heat to medium and stir in the almond paste with ¼ cup (60 ml) ghee. Stir in rest of ghee in ¼-cup (60 ml) increments until all of it has been absorbed. Keep stirring over medium to medium-low heat; mixture will become a single mass and roll around in pan. If mixture begins to brown, lower the heat. Continue stirring until mixture becomes porous and starts to appear drier—this can take up to 10 minutes.

Spread mixture in an ungreased 9-inch (23 cm) square baking pan and press into ½-inch (1½ cm) thickness. Immediately sprinkle with almonds, gently pressing them into the surface. While still warm, cut into 36 squares or diamond shapes.

Serve at room temperature.

<small>PREPARATION: 45 MINUTES, INCLUDING
20 MINUTES TO PREPARE GHEE SERVES: 8 TO 12
YIELD: APPROXIMATELY 36 PIECES</small>

Mysore Pak

I've always been fond of this sweet—an Indian shortbread made with roasted chickpea flour and ghee. Since traditional Indian kitchens don't have ovens, all the sweets are made on a stove. To get the right final texture, pay attention to the visual cues and temperature; I recommend using a candy thermometer. Mysore Pak will keep for up to a week in an airtight container.

1 cup (140g) chickpea flour, sifted

2 cups (380g) sugar

¾ cup (180 ml) water

Ghee (page 172), prepared from 12 ounces
(3 sticks; 340g) unsalted butter and
kept warm

Butter a 9-inch (23 cm) square baking pan.

In a frying pan over medium to medium-high heat, stir sifted chickpea flour until flour turns light golden and gives off a faint toasted aroma. Set aside.

In a heavy 4-quart (4 L) pot combine sugar and water and boil together until candy thermometer registers 220°F (104°C) and a small amount of the syrup, carefully sampled from the stirrer, feels quite gummy between thumb and forefinger.

Add half of warm ghee, stirring as mixture starts to bubble. Add warm chickpea flour gradually, stirring constantly with a wire whisk to break up lumps and to prevent burning. Turn heat down to medium and continue to stir until mixture thickens, 3 to 5 minutes. Add remaining ghee and keep stirring.

Continue stirring as mixture gets thicker and airier. As you stir, mixture will start to pull away from sides of pan until at one point it foams up, expanding to twice its original volume. Quickly turn mixture into buttered baking pan; it should fall out as a mass without sticking to the pan (see note). Gently jiggle the baking pan to spread mixture

A Kerala kitchen

around. After 15 minutes, while still warm, cut it into 36 squares or diamonds, then allow to cool completely before removing from pan.

Note: Timing of removal of mixture from pan is critical, so watch carefully for signs. If frothing and expansion have not started in earnest, finished product will have a dense consistency like fudge. If the frothing has passed its peak, product will be too crumbly. It should harden to consistency of shortbread.

PREPARATION TIME: 40 MINUTES,
INCLUDING 20 MINUTES TO PREPARE GHEE   SERVES: 12
YIELD: 36 PIECES

Sooji Halva

 Sooji *(Hindi for "farina")* makes a fairly firm halva *with a granular texture. Indian mothers like this one because it can be whipped up on short notice. I like it because it's full of raisins and cashews and not too rich tasting. Store in an airtight container for up to 2 days.*

⅓ cup (45g) dark raisins
⅓ cup (45g) broken raw cashew nuts
1 teaspoon Ghee (page 172)

1½ cups (360 ml) water

1 cup (175g) farina (Cream of Wheat)
¼ cup (60 ml) ghee
1 cup (190g) sugar
⅛ teaspoon ground cardamom

Lightly butter an 8-inch (20-cm) square cake pan.

In a small frying pan over medium heat, fry raisins and cashews in 1 teaspoon ghee until lightly golden; set aside.

Bring water to a boil; set aside.

In a wok or frying pan combine farina and ¼ cup (60 ml) ghee. Stir constantly over medium-high heat until light brown spots start to appear. Add reserved hot water and stir, preferably with a wire whisk. When water is mostly absorbed, add sugar, cardamom, and fried raisins and cashews. Continue stirring over medium heat for 1 minute, or until mixture becomes semi-solid.

Transfer mixture to buttered pan, pressing lightly to a thickness of 1 inch (2½ cm), and cut into 25 squares or diamond shapes.

Serve warm or at room temperature.

PREPARATION TIME: 30 MINUTES   SERVES: 8
YIELD: 25 SQUARES

Ras Malai

This elegant dessert of cheese patties soaked in pistachio cream was invented by a Bengali sweetmaker. In adapting this recipe, we substituted baked ricotta squares for homemade cheese patties, simplifying the process immensely. The texture of our squares is slightly different from the original, but the taste is incredibly good. Indian grocery stores sell shelled, skinned pistachios, or skins can be easily removed by blanching.

1 15-ounce (425g) container regular or light
   ricotta cheese
½ cup (100g) sugar

2 cups (480 ml) half-and-half
¼ cup (50g) sugar
5 cardamom pods (optional)
1 tablespoon finely chopped pistachios
   and/or almonds, plus extra for garnish

Preheat oven to 350°F (180°C; mark 4).

In a medium bowl thoroughly combine ricotta cheese and ½ cup (100g) sugar. Spread evenly in an ungreased 8-inch (20 cm) square baking pan. Bake in preheated oven for 1 hour, or until golden brown and firm to the touch.

While cheese is baking, prepare sauce by combining half-and-half, ¼ cup (50g) sugar, cardamom pods (if desired), and nuts in a 4-quart (4 L) saucepan. Bring to a boil; turn heat down to medium and continue to simmer, stirring constantly to avoid boiling over. Cook for 15 minutes or until sauce is reduced to three fourths of its original volume, about 1¼ cups (300 ml). Turn off heat, cover, and set aside.

When cheese has finished baking, immediately cut into 9 squares. After cooling for 15 minutes, transfer squares to a shallow serving dish or individual dessert dishes. Reheat sauce until barely boiling and pour over baked squares. Let stand at least 1 hour.

Garnish with additional chopped nuts before serving.

PREPARATION TIME: 1 HOUR,
PLUS 1 HOUR STANDING TIME   SERVES: 9

Gulab Jamun

 These are tender fried cakes (pictured on page 156) soaked in a cardamom-flavored syrup. Traditionally, the dough is made with khoya *(whole milk boiled down to a solid mass), but our friend Mira's combination of nonfat dry milk and heavy cream is an excellent substitute. The smooth dough is shaped into balls, which are fried, then boiled briefly in hot syrup and left to soak in the syrup at room temperature for an hour or two. The result is a delicate-tasting dessert that makes an attractive presentation.*

2 cups (380g) sugar
3 cups (720 ml) water

¾ cup nonfat dry milk
¼ cup (35g) all-purpose (plain) flour, plus
½ teaspoon baking powder (bicarbonate of soda)
⅓ to ½ cup (80 to 120 ml) heavy cream, as needed

Vegetable oil for deep frying

¼ teaspoon ground cardamom

In a 4-quart (4 L) saucepan prepare a syrup by stirring sugar and water over medium heat until all sugar is dissolved. Transfer one third of syrup to a wide pan (where balls will soak when done) and set aside to cool. Keep remaining syrup in saucepan and set aside.

In a medium bowl combine nonfat dry milk, ¼ cup (35g) flour, and baking powder. Add the heavy cream in small increments—stirring to keep mixture well blended— until smooth dough is formed. Turn dough onto a lightly floured board and knead a few times. Form the dough into 24 smooth, seamless 1-inch (2½ cm) balls; if the seams cannot be smoothed over, batter needs a little more cream.

Heat larger amount of reserved syrup in its saucepan until simmering. Keep over low heat.

In a wok or deep saucepan heat oil to 325°F (165°C). Fry 5 or 6 balls at a time until they turn a reddish-brown color, about 3 minutes. If heat is too high, they will brown quickly on the outside and remain uncooked within.

Unloading bags of tea

Drain balls briefly on paper towels, then transfer to simmering syrup, keeping heat high enough to maintain a slow boil. Boil each group as they are fried and drained for about 1 to 2 minutes until they expand somewhat and feel spongy to the touch. Transfer to cooked syrup in the wide pan.

When all balls are cooked, remove simmering syrup from heat and allow to cool for about 15 minutes. (If syrup gets very thick, thin it with a small amount of hot water.) Stir in the cardamom and add syrup to the soaking balls. Set aside for 2 hours before serving. The balls should have a soft, porous texture. Serve in pairs with a small amount of syrup.

Note: The balls will keep refrigerated in their syrup for days. Warm them up slightly before serving; if syrup is too thick, thin it with a little hot water.

PREPARATION TIME: 40 MINUTES,
PLUS 2 HOURS RESTING TIME
YIELD: ABOUT 20 BALLS

SERVES: 8

Fried Bananas

My aunt makes this with flavorful orange-fleshed bananas for a tea snack in her Kattayam home. Although our bananas don't quite compare, this still makes a rich and irresistible dish (pictured on page 156). I serve it for dessert sprinkled with powdered sugar. You could also accompany the bananas with ice cream.

⅔ cup (100g) rice flour
⅓ cup (50g) all-purpose (plain) flour
¾ to 1 cup (180 to 240 ml) water, as needed
1 tablespoon sugar
1/16 teaspoon salt

Vegetable oil for deep frying
4 firm but ripe bananas, halved lengthwise
    and cut into pieces 3 inches (8 cm) long

Confectioners' (icing) sugar to sift on top
    (optional)

Combine flours, water, sugar, and salt to form a moderately thick batter that will stick to the bananas.

In a wok or deep saucepan heat oil to 350°F (180°C). Dip banana pieces in batter and fry about 6 pieces at a time. The pieces should turn golden on both sides in about 2 minutes. Remove with a slotted spoon to paper towels to drain.

If desired, sift confectioners' (icing) sugar over them just before serving.

PREPARATION TIME: 30 MINUTES   SERVES: 6 TO 8

Spiced Tea

I prefer to make this Mughal-style tea (pictured on page 39) with Indian black tea, which can be purchased at Indian grocery stores, but any black tea will work. It's a very comforting conclusion to a meal.

4 cups (960 ml) water
4 cardamom pods, crushed lightly to
    break pods
4 heaping teaspoons black tea
¾ cup (180 ml) whole milk
⅓ cup (65g) sugar

In a medium saucepan bring water and cardamom pods to a boil. Add tea, milk, and sugar, turn heat down, and simmer for 5 minutes. Strain into individual teacups.

PREPARATION TIME: 10 MINUTES   SERVES: 4 TO 6

Mango Lassi

Lassi is an extremely popular drink in the north. Plain lassi *is made with yogurt and sugar with crushed ice and a few drops of rose water. To make this sweet version (pictured on page 156), I use mango pulp sold at Indian or Hispanic grocery stores and yogurt without stabilizers from health food stores.*

½ cup (120 ml) mango pulp
2 cups (480 ml) plain low-fat yogurt
1 cup (240 ml) water
2 tablespoons sugar

In a blender combine mango pulp, yogurt, water, and sugar and blend for 5 to 10 seconds until well blended and slightly foamy.

Serve in individual glasses with ice.

PREPARATION TIME: 15 MINUTES   SERVES: 4 TO 6

South Indian Coffee

The south is known for its coffee, often served sweetened and diluted with full-cream milk (pictured on page 156). Grown in the hills of South India, the beans are sold freshly roasted. Any French-roasted beans will yield a properly robust brew, provided they are ground finely as for espresso.

9 tablespoons very finely ground dark-
    roasted coffee
2 cups (480 ml) boiling water

3 cups (720 ml) whole milk
¼ cup (50g) granulated sugar

Place coffee in a filter over a coffeepot. Pour in 1 cup (240 ml) boiling water. When first cup has completely soaked through, pour in second cup. Since the grind is very fine, it will take a few minutes for water to drip through.

While coffee is dripping through, in a small saucepan heat milk and sugar until very hot but not yet boiling. Add milk to brewed coffee and serve.

PREPARATION TIME: 10 MINUTES   SERVES: 4 TO 6

Spice Blends and Other Staples

THIS CHAPTER PROVIDES RECIPES used to prepare some of the dishes in this book. In the cases of Garam Masala and Sambar Spice Blend, commercial varieties are sold at Indian grocery stores, but I recommend making up a batch of each and storing in airtight jars (they will keep for over a year). Ghee (page 172) should always be made at home and never purchased. A recipe for coconut milk is included in the event that the canned type is unavailable; however, canned coconut milk, with its rich flavor and thick consistency, is preferable.

Sambar Spice Blend

 This mixture can be used to prepare Sambar (page 68) and Rasam Soup (page 53); it's enough for two recipes of Sambar or twenty-four recipes of Rasam. Commercial sambar powder is sold in Indian grocery stores; if you wish to purchase it, use about two-thirds the amount called for; otherwise, it will be too strong.

4 teaspoons ground coriander
1 teaspoon ground cumin
¼ teaspoon ground red pepper (cayenne)
¼ teaspoon ground black pepper
¼ teaspoon ground turmeric
⅛ teaspoon asafetida

Combine all ingredients thoroughly and store in an airtight jar.

YIELD: ABOUT 2 TABLESPOONS

Garam Masala

This mixture (garam masala means "hot spices" in Hindi) will give you the piquant spice mixture used to round out many North Indian curries. If you use a commercial brand instead, use twice the amount called for, since it will not be as potent.

1 teaspoon ground cinnamon
1 teaspoon ground cloves
1 teaspoon ground cardamom
1 teaspoon ground black pepper

Combine ingredients thoroughly and store in an airtight jar. This mixture will keep for months.

YIELD: ABOUT 1½ TABLESPOONS

Coconut Milk

If canned coconut milk is unavailable, make it from dried grated coconut sold in health food stores or Indian grocery stores. I recommend using a blender because it produces a thicker milk than a food processor. Coconut milk will keep in the freezer for months.

1 cup (115g) finely grated unsweetened coconut
1 cup (240 ml) warm water

Two varieties of coconuts still in their husks

If the coconut is coarsely shredded, process it dry in a blender or food processor until finely grated.

In a blender or food processor, combine coconut with warm water. In blender, process on highest setting for 10 seconds and allow to sit for 10 minutes. (If using a food processor, process coconut and water for at least 30 seconds.)

Place dish towel (tea cloth) or two layers of cheesecloth (muslin) in a colander over a large bowl. Pour coconut into cloth and twist cloth to press out all liquid.

YIELD: ABOUT ¾ CUP (180 ML)

Ghee

 Ghee *is butter that has been slowly heated so that all the moisture evaporates and all the milk solids turn to sediment. It keeps for at least a month at room temperature, an important feature in India, where refrigeration is a recent luxury. Although prepared* ghee *is available at Indian grocery stores, the flavor is far superior when it's made at home. Store* ghee *in a tightly covered opaque container. It solidifies at room temperature, with a slightly granular consistency; to melt it for serving, place it next to the burners while you're cooking, or place the container in a few inches of hot water.*

8 ounces (2 sticks; 225g) butter

In a heavy skillet over medium to medium-low heat, heat butter until completely melted. Watch as butter boils, first with large bubbles and white milk solids floating on the surface, then with only a fine white foam filling entire surface. Stir occasionally.

Soon small patches of golden brown will appear on the surface, and overall color of butter will change from yellow to golden. Push aside foam periodically to check color of sediment. When sediment turns light brown, remove from heat (see note).

Decant into a jar with a tight lid. Warm, if desired, for serving over rice.

Note: If you heat until sediment turns dark brown, ghee will lose its flavor and taste like vegetable oil.

PREPARATION TIME: 20 TO 25 MINUTES
YIELD: ABOUT 1 CUP

Paneer

This basic recipe for preparing the homemade cheese used in Spinach Paneer (page 81) and Peas Paneer (page 80) yields the best texture with whole milk; skim milk makes it too firm. Fried paneer may be made ahead of time and refrigerated.

2 quarts (1,900 ml) whole milk

¼ cup (60 ml) lemon juice

Vegetable oil for deep frying

In a large, deep pot over medium-high heat, heat milk. As soon as it reaches a full boil and foams up, remove from heat and stir in lemon juice. Milk will split into curds and whey.

Pour contents of pot into cheesecloth (muslin) or dish towel (tea cloth) placed inside a colander. When cool enough to handle, gently twist cloth to squeeze out most of the liquid. Scrape milk solids together into ball. Keeping it wrapped in the cloth, flatten ball into a ½-inch (1½ cm) disc and set on a cookie sheet (baking tray). Place a heavy pan partially filled with water (about 2 to 3 pounds [900 to 1,350g] of weight) on top of disc. Let stand for 2 hours at room temperature until cheese becomes a flat slab.

In a wok or deep saucepan heat oil to 350°F (180°C).

While oil heats, unwrap slab and cut into a roughly ½-inch (1½ cm) dice. Deep-fry cheese dice, half at a time, in oil until light golden. Remove with a slotted spoon to paper towels to drain.

PREPARATION TIME: 20 MINUTES TO MAKE CHEESE; 2 HOURS TO COMPRESS; 20 MINUTES TO FRY

YIELD: ABOUT 2 CUPS CUBED PANEER, ENOUGH FOR ONE RECIPE PEAS PANEER OR SPINACH PANEER

Menu Planning

MOST OF THE CURRIES and rice dishes in this book feed 6 to 8 people when 3 to 5 curries are served. If the gathering is over 8 people, serve more than one meat, fish, chicken, or egg dish. ◻ Consider removing pieces of whole seasonings like split green chilies, dried red chilies, and cinnamon sticks before serving a curry. People usually push them to the side of their plate, but removing them from the dish avoids any unpleasant surprises. ◻ When selecting a beverage to serve, think of pale ales or Indian lagers. Wine is a good alternative, especially a Riesling with its sweet and spicy flavors. ◻ Numerals refer to page numbers on which these recipes can be found.

BREAKFASTS

Rava Idli (30) or Rava Dosa (32), Coconut Chutney (58), Sambar (68), South Indian Coffee (169)

Upuma (29), sliced bananas, South Indian Coffee (169)

Spicy Scrambled Eggs (36) or Tomato and Onion Omelettes (37), toast, Mango Lassi (169), Spiced Tea (168)

TEA SNACK COMBINATIONS

Samosas (46), Baji (43), Tamarind Chutney (59), Shami Kabab (45), Chutney for Kabab (61)

Split Pea Vada (38), Potato Vada (40), Coconut Chutney (58), Fried Bananas (168)

Bonda (42), Coconut Chutney (58), Meat Cutlets (44), Spicy Tomato Chutney (61), Mysore Pak (162)

LUNCHES OR LIGHT DINNERS

Chicken-Fry (115), Potatoes and Onions with Tomatoes (88), Appam (34)

Meat Cutlets (44), Tomato and Onion Salad (56), Potato Stew (87), Appam (34)

Rava Masala Dosa (33), Bonda (42), Coconut Chutney (58), Sambar (68)

Lamb Stew with Potatoes (129), Rava Dosa (32), Tomato and Cucumber Salad (56)

Kerala Fried Fish (103), Spinach Dhal (67), Aviyal (70), Ginger Yogurt (57), Long-Grain Rice (144)

Egg Aviyal (125), Stir-Fried Okra (78), Tomato Pachadi (83), Long-Grain Rice (144), Pappadam (49)

Sambar (68), Cabbage Thoren (73), Spinach Pachadi (82), Coconut Rice (146), Pappadam (49)

Chicken Tikka (121), Cholé (93), Tomato and Cucumber Salad (56), Chappathi (154)

Lamb Kabab (134), Potatoes and Onions (86), Raita (57), Basmati Rice (145), Puri (152)

Fish with Mustard Seeds (105), Potatoes and Cauliflower with Peas (91), Tomato and Onion Salad with Yogurt (56), Long-Grain Rice (144)

Lamb or Chicken Biriyani (150), Tomato and Cucumber Salad (56), Ginger Yogurt (57), Pappadam (49)

VEGETARIAN COMBINATIONS

Rasam (53), Spicy Dhal with Tomatoes (66), Peas Thoren (76), Potato Korma (92), Long-Grain Rice (144), Ghee (172), Pappadam (49), Milk Payasam (159)

Sambar (68) or Kootu (69), Stir-Fried Okra (78), Potatoes and Bell Peppers (90), Tomato and Onion Salad (56), Lemon Rice (147), yogurt

Spinach Dhal (67), Green Beans Thoren (75), Sweet Potato Erisheri (72), Aviyal (70), Ginger Yogurt (57), Long-Grain Rice (144), Ghee (172), Pappadam (49), Vermicelli Payasam (160)

Spinach Paneer (81), Chickpeas with Mushrooms (94), Raita (57), Long-Grain Rice (144), Puri (152), Ras Malai (165)

Guidelines for Full-Scale Dinners

Create a menu for a large dinner by choosing items from the following groups. Be sure the curries you pick offer a variety of color and consistency.

Soup/First Course: Rasam, Pulisheri, or Mulligatawny

Meat Curry: Any meat, chicken, fish, or egg curry

Legumes: Any *dahl*, Sambar, or Kootu

Light Vegetable: Any *thoren* or stir-fried vegetable

Rich Vegetable: Any potato, eggplant, *paneer,* or chickpea curry

Salad: A *pachadi,* a *kichadi,* any tomato salad, Raita, or Ginger Yogurt

Rice: Either plain served with Ghee and Pappadam, or a flavored rice dish (except Biriyani)

Last Course: Any dessert or fruit

Sources for Ingredients

United States

Adriana's Caravan
Brooklyn, New York
800-316-0820
Mail order only

Kalustyan, Orient Export Trading Corporation
123 Lexington Avenue
New York, New York 10016
212-685-3451

Patel Brothers
Flushing, New York
718-321-9847
Mail order only

Jay Store
6688 Southwest Freeway
Houston, Texas 77074
713-783-0032

Culinary Alchemy
San Francisco, California
415-367-1455
Mail order only

Australia

Moses Spice Centre
108 Brighton Boulevarde
Bondi Beach, NSW 3026
612-30-3234

France

V. S. Company Cash and Carry
197 Rue du Faubourg
Saint Denis 75010 Paris
1-40-34-71-65

Japan

Hillside Pantry
Hillside Terrace G-B1
18–12, Sarugaku-cho
Shibuya-ku, Tokyo
03-34-96-6620

United Kingdom

The Spice Shop
1 Blenheim Crescent
London W11 2EE
171-221-4448

Index

Index 🮇 179

Bibliography

Achaya, K. T. *Indian Food: A Historical Companion.* Oxford, England: Oxford University Press, 1994.

Atwood, Mary S. *A Taste of India.* New York: Avon Books, 1969.

Burton, David. *The Raj at the Table.* London: Faber and Faber, 1994.

Crowther, Geoff, Prakash A. Raj, Tony Wheeler, Hugh Finlay, and Bryn Thomas. *India, A Travel Survival Kit.* Fifth Edition. Berkeley, Calif.: Lonely Planet, 1993.

Devi, Yamuna. *Lord Krishna's Cuisine: The Art of Indian Vegetarian Cooking.* New York: Dutton, 1987.

Dewitt, Dave, and Arthur Pais. *A World of Curries.* Boston: Little, Brown and Company, 1994.

Jaffrey, Madhur. *A Taste of India.* New York: Atheneum, 1988.

Mathew, K. M. *Kerala Cookery.* Kottayam, India: Manorama Publishing House, 1964.

————. *Modern Kerala Dishes.* Kottayam, India: Yamuna Press, 1979.

Norman, Jill. *The Complete Book of Spices.* New York: Penguin Books, 1995.

Patnaik, Naveen. *The Garden of Life: An Introduction to the Healing Plants of India.* New York: Doubleday, 1993.

Rau, Santha Rama. *The Cooking of India.* New York: Time-Life Books, 1969.

Sahni, Julie. *Classic Indian Cooking.* New York: William Morrow and Company, 1980.

Singh, Dharamjit. *Indian Cookery.* New York: Penguin Books, 1984.

Sokolov, Raymond. *Why We Eat What We Eat.* New York: Simon & Schuster, 1993.

Varughese, B. F. *Recipes for All Occasions.* Kottayam, India: Panampunna, 1994.

Visser, Margaret. *The Rituals of Dinner.* New York: Penguin Books, 1992.

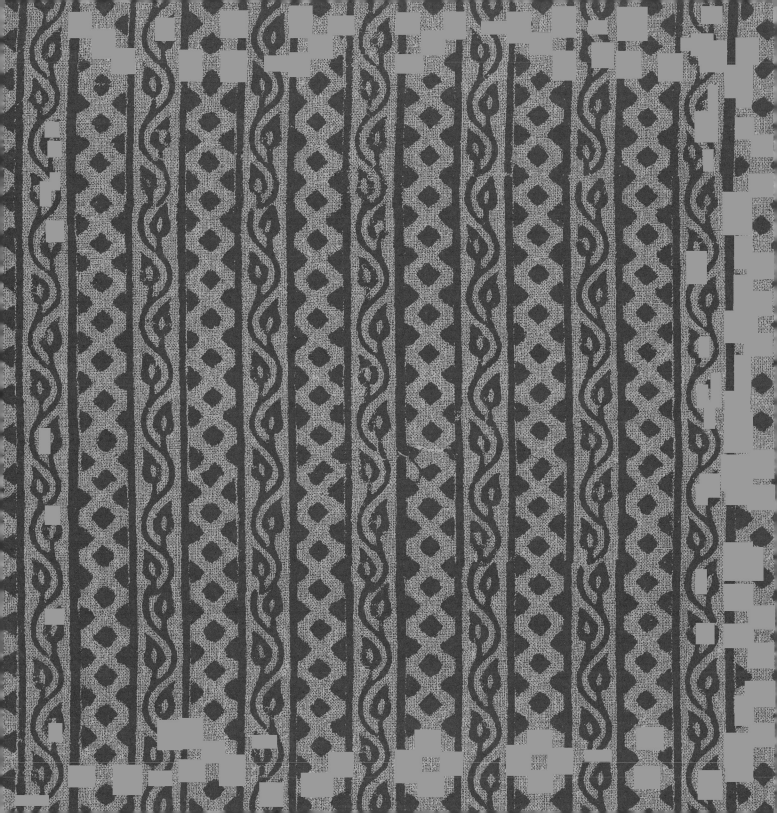